Dream Catcher 49

Stairwell Books //

Dream Catcher 49

SUBSCRIPTIONS TO
DREAM CATCHER
MAGAZINE

£15.00 UK (Two issues inc. p&p)
£22.00 Europe
£25.00 USA and Canada

Cheques should be made
payable to **Dream Catcher**
and sent to:

Dream Catcher Subscriptions
161 Lowther Street
York, YO31 7LZ
UK

+44 1904 733767

argillott@gmail.com

www.dreamcatchermagazine.co.uk
@literaryartsmag
www.stairwellbooks.co.uk
@stairwellbooks

Dream Catcher Magazine

Dream Catcher No. 49

ISSN: 1466-9455

Published by Stairwell Books //

ISBN: 978-1-913432-95-9

p8

Contents – Authors

Featured Artist *Karen Krieger* 1
Editorial 3
In Conversation With... Bob Beagrie 4
A Mammal's Notebook *Bob Beagrie* 9
The Trade Off *Bob Beagrie* 10
The Hand in Renaissance Painting *Bob Beagrie* 11
Naisho *Bob Beagrie* 12
Camera Obscura *Graham Mort* 13
35MM *Oz Hardwick* 15
Night Cries *Keith Willson* 16
Bride or Broom *Simon Tindale* 17
Once Upon a Time *Ruth Aylett* 18
The Return *Colin Pink* 19
Raising the Ghosts *Kemal Houghton* 20
The Small Print *Estill Pollock* 21
Elegy Written in a North Country Churchyard *George Jowett* 23
Loop *Estill Pollock* 24
Death Hangs Around *Tonnie Richmond* 26
Inheritance *Anne Eyries* 27
All Action Hero *David Thompson* 28
Baby Formula 1 *David Thompson* 29
Midnight Pacing *David Thompson* 30
Finally, Chopin *David Sapp* 31
Father at 6 a.m. *Hilaire* 33
The Family Man Who Lives in Boxes *Moira Garland* 34
The Hand of a Woman *Steve Smith* 38
Two Pictures *David Sapp* 41
Thomas Writes His Sister's Name *Phil Connolly* 43
Thomas and the Birthday Stones *Phil Connolly* 44
Jonathan Arthur *Anne Ryland* 46
Zoom *Stuart Pickford* 47
In Sheltered Accommodation *Michael Newman* 48
Leeds Bus Station *William Coniston* 49
Blackthorn Stick *Simon Haines* 50
Committed *Simon Tindale* 51

Asylum *Margaret Poynor-Clark* 52

The Merman Indigo *Martha Glaser* 53

The Fisherman's Lure *Guy Jones* 57

A Snail's Pace Beam of Light *Philip Dunn* 59

Key Points in Evolution *Oz Hardwick* 60

Indian Fragments *Susan Sciama* 61

The Thomas Hardy Sat. Nav. *Martin Reed* 62

Tracey Emin's Shoe, Folkestone *Hilaire* 63

Kurt Cobain in Whitely Bay *Ian Chapman* 64

Stags and Hens *Ruth Aylett* 65

Great Stuart Street *Anne Ryland* 66

A Tea Shop in Bandon *Owen O'Sullivan* 68

In Amsterdam *Katie Campbell* 69

The Visitor to the Mountain Refuge *Clifford Liles* 70

Party on Scutchamer Knob *Ivan McGuinness* 71

When *Andy Fletcher* 72

Autumn Pudding *Martin Reed* 73

Delicatessen *Ruth Aylett* 74

Basket Case *Ken Gambles* 75

Millet *John Andrew* 76

Beetroot *Stuart Pickford* 77

Harvest *Ivan McGuinness* 78

Not to be Found in Any Rainbow *Gerald Killingworth* 79

Bamboozled in May *Owen O'Sullivan* 80

Red Grouse *Greg Smith* 81

Red Bird Spotted by Z-Gen Youth *Corbett Buchly* 82

To a Fly *Greg Smith* 83

Event Horizon *Oz Hardwick* 84

The Curvature of the Earth from South London *Bel Wallace* 85

Making Our First Ever Cup of Tea *Katie Campbell* 87

Where I Must Have Put the Thing *James B. Nicola* 88

The I Way *Terry Sherwood* 89

Excuse Me *Anne Eyries* 91

The Search for My Body *Heather Hughes* 92

The House Hides the Body and Collapses onto It *Heather Hughes* 93

Blade & Bomb *Colin Pink* 94

The Garden at Castlecountess *Noel King* 95

Moonset *James B. Nicola* 96

Shadow on the Moon *Terry Sherwood*   97

Sea Sky Land *Colin Pink*   98

A Climate of Hostility *Wilf Deckner*   99

Fern *Debi Knight*   100

Wintering *Andria Cooke*   101

The Canopy *Andria Cooke*   102

An Hour with Misha *Heather Deckner*   103

Professors *Niall McGrath*   104

Young Ascherson *George Jowett*   105

The Grandmaster *Mark Pearce*   106

Wizard *Niall McGrath*   109

The Church of St. John the Dentist *Malcolm Carson*   110

Camels on Long Island *Katie Campbell*   111

'She Wears Her Clothes, as If They Were Thrown on with a Pitchfork' *Hilaire*   114

The Gaze *Jagoda Olender*   115

Friendships Are Complicated *Jagoda Olender*   116

End *William Coniston*   117

The Third Step *Stuart Pickford*   118

Contents of My Pocket *Carmella de Keyser*   119

Lunch Hour in the Stationery Cupboard *Simon Tindale*   120

Our Castles *Anne Ryland*   121

Three Little Pigs *Daniel Souza*   122

Gracie *Moira Garland*   126

Crashed Last Night *Bel Wallace*   129

Building Me *Joe Spivey*   130

Jack Green *John Andrew*   131

Reviews   133

Eftwyrd by Bob Beagrie *Hannah Stone*   133

A to Z of Superstitions by Ian Harker *Patrick Lodge*   134

In Search of a Subject by John Short *Pauline Kirk*   135

Games of Soldiers by Mary Michaels *Hannah Stone*   137

All the Eyes that I have Opened by Franca Mancinelli (translated by John Taylor) *Patrick Lodge*   138

Are You Judging Me Yet? Poetry and Everyday Sexism by Kim Moore *Hannah Stone*   140

The Invisible by Alessio Zanelli *Nick Allen*   141

Index of Authors   143

FEATURED ARTIST
ARTIST STATEMENT: KAREN KRIEGER

Poets help us see the world and its incongruence. Milton lost the ability to see the words he was writing. Emily Dickinson, the master of miniature detail, lasered in on the 'best things', the things that are out of sight, hidden away in her 'Best Things dwell out of Sight', quoted here in full:

> Best Things dwell out of Sight
> The Pearl – the Just – Our Thought.
> Most shun the Public Air
> Legitimate, and Rare –
> The Capsule of the Wind
> The Capsule of the Mind
> Exhibit here, as doth a Burr –
> Germ's Germ be where?

Boston based painter Karen Krieger seems to share this concern for that, though hidden, interconnects seemingly disparate aspects of the world around us: the linear and the iridescent; the edge and the cavity, the clarity and the murk. This is not to, in the style of many modern art critics, simply list dichotomous elements and sit back, basking in a bovine culturality. Krieger's art demands more than that, as does the reader of this very poetryzine. What we're faced with here is an invitation to make sense of the world around us, indeed to go further. When we look at something, do we really see it? In a postmodern world, where the maelstrom of visual half-truths and AI generated fakes is blinding, have we learned to discriminate?

Krieger's art, all experimental mark making and Chinese Ink, skewers the natural environment in a series of mountainscapes, opening up space for contemplation in the tradition of all the best painters and indeed poets. The goal here is not representation but rather a questioning. If we look closely at the visual surface of a mountain, why do we try and impose a monolithic quality that belies its true wriggling, water bejewelled nature? Krieger seems to have reached the same Damascus moment experienced by John Ruskin (who would have surely approved of her depictions of the natural world). In 1851 Ruskin walked through the uplands of the Jura. He finds an unexpected silent landscape, 'no whisper, nor patter, nor murmur'. He keeps walking, over 'absolutely crisp turf and sun bright rock without so much water anywhere as a crest could grow in or a tadpole wag his tail in.' A rain cloud passes and drenches the waterless land, yet within an hour the rocks are dry again. He looks closely and sees, and discloses his findings in almost breathless writing. This quiet plateau he finds is riddled with 'unseen fissures and filmy crannies'. Into these the waters vanish, and 'far away, down in the depths of the main valley, glides the strong river, unconscious.' Unlike many of us who see only the colour of the flags or

the tribalism of people's politics, Ruskin was achingly aware of the ecosystems that interconnect the real world, the world depicted by Karen Krieger, a world where cumulus clouds are as crenelated as the chasm they half conceal. One is not distinct from the other. The structure of the earth has a natural theology, and if you'll allow me to stretch the point, there is more fertility in the intersection that connects us than that which demarcates. If Ruskin was to have painted his Eureka moment his creation may have looked a little like that of Karen Krieger's. Emily Dickinson's 'capsule of the wind', hitherto unseen, is discernible in such interfusion of that which we may initially dismiss as disparity.
Greg McGee

PAGES OF ARTWORK

Snow Wave Mountains 3	*Cover*
Cosmic Ocean	22
Dawn Unfolding	45
Ice Cliff Ledge	67
Silent Cliff Pass	90
Snow Obscured Heights	113

I can't help being aware that poets who jolly us along with assurances that if winter comes, spring is on its heels, would put it quite differently if writing during the closing days of the Anthropocene. This is our 'summer' issue, but with the honourable exception of a few warmer days, Yorkshire has so far escaped much manifestation that we have emerged from the colder season. All the more reason to consume the writings of imaginative souls who create their own weather, or observe climactic changes of both personal and cosmic significance. Whatever our unease about how humans are behaving in the days of climate change, at least our creativity is keeping AI at bay (or is it …?).

Deciding on a sequence for the selected content of any one issue is, for sure, the most enjoyable aspect of editing this journal. I am ably assisted in this by Daisy, my rescue cat, who not only draws my attention to the envelopes that arrive on the doormat below her catflap (preferably during the submission 'windows', please, and NOT recorded delivery), but then sits on the contents of said envelopes, once they are spread out on the sitting room floor, as I marshal them into a pleasing order, like some oracle, whose tail twitches must be correctly read. Of course, I honour also the contributions of the human editorial team who work so hard reading and reviewing submissions. Thank you for all you do.

It's rare that we fail to get poems about the natural world, stories about family relationships, discussions of global politics, and writing that is not necessary primarily *about* anything but simply putting language through a work out, testing its limits. But how often do you read an ode to a fly? Meet Kurt Cobain in Whitley Bay? Read a lesson plan for anger management? Find black holes in your pockets? Read on.

In DC 48 I mentioned the concept of a poetry manifesto (am I the only poet who gets asked not only why I write but what should poetry *do*, as if it had to justify its existence by having SMART targets?). It was one of the questions I raised with Bob Beagrie, who is my first guest in a new feature for Dream Catcher, which I'm calling 'In conversation with ….'. For a number of years I ran a live event (then covid-ified podcast) for the Leeds Library called Nowt but Verse, in which I discussed with a fellow poet not only their current work, but their ideas about poetry, their influences and future plans. In agreement with the rest of the editorial team, I felt this would transfer well to the page. Having heard Bob perform his lushly hybrid work, accompanied by musicians using home-made instruments (provoking more questions that it would be polite to ask in just one evening), I invited him to be my first subject. I hope you enjoy this new content.

Hannah Stone

HS   Bob, thanks so much for being our very first poet 'in conversation' with the editor of Dream Catcher. We've really enjoyed publishing your work in previous issues, and I was delighted to have the opportunity to review *Eftwyrd* in this current issue. I get the feeling that your work speaks from historical contexts but also for the present day. Can you explain how this came about and give us a thumb nail sketch of your most recent publications, to put them into the historical/political context?

BB   I do tend to write a lot from a historical context, but it's with an awareness that history is not some 'other' discourse removed from the lived experiences of ordinary people. It shouldn't be solely concerned with Kings and Queens or Middlesbrough's Ironmasters or great explorers; nor is it simply confined to the past but composed from the ongoing 'stuff' of our daily lives. It thereby raises and counters the sense of marginalisation and disenfranchisement from 'official' history, society and politics. Our lived experiences are very much a result of the historical conditions from which the present forms itself. A lot of my poetry explores tumultuous paradigm shifts within the culture of Northern England but it does so by focussing upon ordinary people caught up in and struggling to adapt to the changes taking place, capturing the commonplace, mundane experiences as well as the internal and external conflicts people face. By doing so I try to connect the reader's own sensory memories to the historic timeline.

So *Endeavour: Newfound Notes* (2004) is a long poem which describes James Cook's first voyage to Tahiti and then into the Southern Ocean to discover New Zealand and map Western Australia, but it is told from a young enlisted seaman's perspective who, unlike Cook, didn't get the education and apprenticeship, and is his kind of doppleganger. *Leásungspell* (2016) and *Eftwyrd* (2023) are both set in 7th Century Northumbria during the long conversion from paganism to Christianity and also covers the tensions between Celtic and Roman Christianity which came to a head in Whitby in AD 664, but again the focus is on a lowly monk of little standing and the people he meets as he travels from Hartlepool to Whitby. *Civil Insolencies* (2019) explores the ruptures in identity that came to a head in the British Civil Wars, but I use the Battle of Guisborough as a kind of microscope to examine the interactions and social dynamics between a cast of ordinary people swept up in it all. My new collection, *Romanceros: poems inspired by the Spanish Civil War* focuses on the working-class men and women (particularly those from Teesside) who decided to go to Spain to support the Spanish Republic against the rise of Fascism under Franco supported by Mussolini and Hitler. So, I am very much interested in people's history and see poetry as a way of bringing that to life in a visceral way to remind us that we too are faced with the same dilemmas, carry our own illusions and prejudices and wrangle with our own consciences.

HS   Thank you; it seems that this historical context is not purely determined by a focus on, and certainly does not present, a romanticisation of the past. It feels like your purpose in writing in this way is to shine a spotlight on contemporary political and social issues, but without writing a personal rant: am I right?

BB   Yes, very much so. By examining the past we are often able to see the present with clearer vision, so the epic poems I've written that deal with these historical conflicts also shed light and comment upon the social and political forces within our contemporary moment. It is no accident that *Civil Insolencies* was published in 2019 after several years of bitter divisions over Brexit, the rise of cultural intolerance, populist politics and radically combative visions of what Britain should become. *Romanceros* highlights the historical parallels between 1936 and what is going on in the world now, the global tensions, the vast and growing gap in living standards between the majority and a small, entitled elite, the political hypocrisy, unbridled propaganda and the slaughter of innocent people. In my PhD thesis I unpick this narrative / poetic strategy and give it the name 'Pan-Temporal Parallelism'.

HS   That would make for fascinating reading! I'm especially interested in your use of hybrid language; for example, the combinations of dialect and Anglo-Saxon, not least because of the *sound* of the words. The first time I saw you perform you read to a backing track of music, and I was very struck by that. Can you say something about these experiments in hybrid vernacular languages? Do they owe something in particular to oral culture?

BB   Definitely. A lot of my poetry tries to capture the energy of spoken Northern English vernacular. I have a very strong Teesside accent and my poetry has often attempted to give it a literary legitimacy by embracing and utilizing the richness and quirkiness of dialect. I am fascinated by the effects of discourses clashing within a text and often purposefully experiment with Bakhtin's notions of heteroglossia and polyphony.

HS   As I mention in my review, when reading *Eftwyrd* I soon found myself gravitating to the left-hand page, where the hybrid language appears. To assist in comprehension as well as sneaky glances to the facing page, I found reading it out loud really helped. Do you have any particular desires or suggestions for readers who meet your work for the first time?

BB   The distortion of language within *Leásungspell* and *Eftwyrd* is taken to quite an extreme. Having read various novels set in the Early Middle Ages, I found their representations of a pre-Enlightenment world-view unconvincing, as if the characters were modern and simply in costume, against a backdrop of the historical period. To more authentically render the mythopoeic mindset of the narrator and characters I found it necessary to defamiliarize the language through a process of experimentation with vocabulary and syntax, thereby foregrounding its historical 'otherness' to modern interpretative strategies. This led to a balancing act between legibility and creative authenticity.

Given the lack of surviving 7th Century Northumbrian I used Old English spellings and obsolete letters from the Old English alphabet and drew upon the conventions of an essentially oral language, informed by the poetic principles underpinning Old English verse such as kennings, riddles, aphorisms, metaphorical listings, alliteration, and consonantal anaphora. Idioms and expressions from Northumbrian, Yorkshire and Cleveland dialect forms are used, and slang terms from modern day vernaculars are also woven through. Vocabulary choice involved etymological research and decisions to select, where possible, words with a Germanic rather than Latinate root.

Through the layering of historical, linguistic and poetic experimentation the text reclaims and dignifies a 'bygonese' based on Anglo Saxon and Northen dialects. In doing so *Leásungspell* and *Eftwyrd* represent a creative reimagining of a lost language whose ghosts still haunt twenty first century English(es). Dr Claire Hélie, a French academic, has termed the linguistic and syntactic experimentation within *Leásungspell* as a process of "rewilding language." (Claire Hélie, Conference paper, 'Bob Beagrie's Northern Bygonese in *Leásungspell* ' for the European Society for the Study of English 15th Annual Conference, 02 September 2021).

How does the reader cope with the mash-up of languages, use of fragmentation and hybridity? Initially it may appear unintelligible, however a glossary of terms and guide to pronunciation is included in *Leasungspell*, and in *Eftwyrd* most of the archaic texts have a facing page translation (although not all) and with these, upon closer inspection and a degree of 'openness' (Keats's 'Negative Capability') and a willingness to interpret it through oral phonetics, a greater degree of familiarity emerges. Like the hybrid languages used in Russell Hoban's *Riddley Walker* (1980*)*, Anthony Burgess' *A Clockwork Orange* (1962), and in the heavily dialect-based rendering of Glaswegian in Irvine Welsh's *Trainspotting* (1993), with patience and a little perseverance the general reader is able to 'tune in' to the idiosyncrasies so that it becomes largely legible whilst retaining its 'otherness'. This is also aided by the relatively limited diction employed and the adoption of phrasal repetition, a defining feature within the formulaic apparatus of oral verse forms and which reinforces the text's compositional verisimilitude to the oral poetics of pre-literate epics.

HS I've always been a big fan of Keats' 'Negative Capability' – a phrase taken from one of his letters to his brother, where he talks about his attempt to be 'in uncertainties, mysteries, doubts, without any irritable reaching after fact or reason.' And the idea of 'rewilding language' seems so pertinent today, as an antidote to the nasty narrowness and sterility of so much of British so-called culture. Further to these ideas, do you have any sense of a poetry 'manifesto', i.e. what you think poetry 'should' do? Does it have a 'job', or certain responsibilities? Many other poets have expressed quite strident opinions about this, often through the lens of what they hope *their* poetry will communicate!

BB   As for a manifesto, well not really, but I do have a sense of poetry as belonging to the people and see it as an act of participatory resistance to the homogeneity of mainstream mass media. I see it in an anchored bardic sense that it transforms the inchoate experiences of life into some kind of pattern that we are then able to share and compare and contrast with others to find a sense of meaning and identity. This is happening in the many vibrant communities of writers and poets in so many places who meet at live events and workshops and writers' groups, but which is all but invisible to anyone who isn't already involved, it all goes on under the radar. It also links to Patrick Kavanagh's concept of the Parochial Imagination which is never in any doubt about the social and artistic validity of his own parish. I also like the more recent idea of 'International Regionalism' developed by John Kinsella as a poetic critique of centralisation within increasing globalisation. So, while my own poetry does shift about a great deal in terms of time and temporality it is all firmly rooted in a sense of place. What has emerged over several decades of playing with this approach is the realisation of the potential of localised mythologies' ability to undermine 'disenchanted' alienation. How they can instil a sense of belonging and connectedness to a particular place. Like the Irish Dindsenchas, this kind of creative reimagining of place can be seen as instrumental in cultivating 'folk memory'.

HS   In addition to poets you have already mentioned, and the heritage of various regional vernacular poetries, are there particular poets, living or departed, who influence your practice, and what would you like to say to them about your work?

BB   There are many other poets that have shaped my practice, but I see Ted Hughes and Basil Bunting's *Briggflatts*, also Ken Smith and Tony Harrison are core influences. Derek Walcott's *Omeros* and his *Apple Star Kingdom* made a massive impression on me in terms of their scale and ambition and rootedness. In terms of epic revisioning of mythic, historical and contemporary elements, there is also obviously W.B. Yeats, and more recently Brendan Kennelly, Anne Carson, Margaret Atwood, Steve Ely, Martin Malone, Jane Burn, Alice Oswald. I think there is a fascinating renewal of interest in the epic as a form which is able to tackle big societal questions and allows the poet to move beyond personal expression and individual consciousness. This blending of mythical, historical and contemporary features in poetry is also something I examine in my thesis and which I call 'Historio-mythography' and argue that it is in fact an intrinsic aspect of the epic poem, one of the key functions of which is to enact and illustrate ruptures to the symbolic order of collective identification.

HS   Tell us a bit more about what we are going to read in this issue of Dream Catcher, from your latest work. And can you say anything about your process in writing; do you start with a word or phrase, an idea, a shape? Do you carry a notebook around or make voice notes?

BB   I do carry a notebook and I am often just scribbling away in it randomly, collecting observations, snippets of ideas and bits of overheard conversations. It is what I call composting, most of it won't be used but sometimes you look back on the notes and find something oddly striking about a phrase or an image that then grows into a poem. Once an idea starts to shape I tend to get a bit obsessed with it.

The four pieces here are from a new sequence of prose poems I've been working on called *The Hand of Glory: a biography*. I've written fifty-five pieces so far which are playful, surreal and often absurd imaginings of the adventures and exploits of the dismembered human hand on display in Whitby Museum. It's claimed it is the last Hand of Glory in existence in Britain at least. They were supposedly cut from the body of a hanged felon and dried, while being subject to various spells to imbue it with magical powers and used in nefarious practices such as burglary. There's quite a lot of fascinating folklore about the hand of glory and it crops up in various stories and films, but the sequence also explores the dismembered hand in a wider symbolic sense as well as referencing Thing from *The Addams Family*, Luke Skywalker's severed hand, Ash's severed hand from *The Evil Dead*, The Society of the Black Hand, The Buddha's palm, the secret society of assassins known as The Hand from Marvel Comics. It has been fun and a bit of light relief after the heavy and often distressing process of research and writing that informed *Romanceros*.

HS   thank you so much, Bob, for responding to my interrogation and we look forward very much to reading your work, both here and in the new book.

Relief was a family household with all its quirks and curiosities, its entrenched rituals and unspoken rivalries, its trapdoors, tripwires, locked chests, its generational undercurrents of compound custom and lore. According to a recently discovered diary the hand flourished there, slept in a purple velvet lined box, became a pet for a little girl. Dancer, entertainer, secret sleuth to spy on her brother, roaming ninja-like among rafters, lurking in cobwebbed corners, messenger, guardian, would-be rescuer. Together they mastered fingerspelling and Morse code to weave wicked tales of prepubescent woe, thrilled by terrors never felt before. She taught him to accompany her as she played piano. Their fingers conjured obscure sorrows of unknowable inner lives, leading Gnossiennes, step by step, note by note, through the labyrinth Theseus believes he can leave alive by following Ariadne's thread.

Bob Beagrie

There was a time, at the height of success, when our charming hand took the hand of a young, wide-eyed bride who liked to trace the tip of her index finger in spirals upon the calloused palm, *round and round the garden like a...* and it was much in love. It lavished her with gifts: perfumes, flowers, dresses, jewellery, shoes, horses, luxurious city breaks and rural retreats. One evening in Shangri La, with its Savile Row suit hung in the wardrobe while it slept, she lay upon the bed reading Collette by the light of a veiled conch the colour of periwinkle. Turning a page, her gaze settled on the sleeping hand, its tendons, lumps, faint scars, and fur, the manicured nails – the perfectly polished crescent moon of each cuticle. She thought of all the previous successes, conquests, victories, ghouls sealed in dungeons: the papers signed, the keys turned in locks, the deals struck, the cities felled to rubble, the woodlands cleared, the plagues cast on kings, the fevers bred, pandemics spread, orders barked, blood spilled, each deathly harvest counted. She caught her breath and stared and stared at the slumbering beast.

Bob Beagrie

Sometimes the hand is placed upon the chest, or else the hand rests on the flank, otherwise the hand points upward to the sky or downward to the earth as if in blessing, or perhaps the hand is shown grasping an object or holding a person. Aside from these common positions there are times when it is seemingly caught mid-gesture, curiously contorted as if surreptitiously photographed rather than painstakingly painted, enacting a secret sign possibly conveying esoteric meanings. The unnatural hand position is likely an artistic device or a symbolic hallmark rather than a pathologic depiction of syndactyly which appears in hundreds of paintings by artists such as Titian, Bronzino, El Greco, Parmigianino, François Clouet, Hans Memling, Anton Raphael Mengs and Luis el Divino Morales, whose subjects adopt this awkward position. Some scholars speculate that the gesture was a physical sign conveying satanic connections, membership to masonic guilds, cryptic cults, sibylline sects or to the society of the Illuminati. The hand forms a well-known shape in which the thumb with the second and third fingers are held touching each other and separated from the fourth and the fifth fingers, conceiving a fan of sorts, not dissimilar to the Kohanic Benediction. Others have pointed out that it resembles a gesture recommended by Saint Ignacio de Loyola, the first Superior General of the Jesuits' Order, to be carried out as part of believer's spiritual devotions while adhering to the motto *perinde ac cadaver* – "as if a dead body".

Bob Beagrie

The Yamaguchi-gumi tell the tale of Sūn Wù Kōng the monkey king who wanted to become Lord of the Sky. The king of monkeys acquired seventy-two earthly transformations, each giving him access to a unique power including transforming into animals and objects, making copies of himself, partial weather manipulation skills, the power to stop people in place with fixing magic and the strength to carry the weight of two mountains on his shoulders while running with the speed of a meteor. With such wonderous abilities it was hardly surprising that the Emperor of Primates caused no end of mischief to the established order, bringing great ruin to many and even rebelling against Heaven. How, in the end, the Lord Buddha had to strike a deal with the Monkey King, saying that if he could leap out of his hand, he would be granted the title of Lord of the Sky. Sūn Wù Kōng laughed his best villainous laugh while stroking the long hairs of his moustache. *That is no contest at all!* he claimed and jumped in a single leap over the mountains and islands and seas to the very edge of the world. There the five red pillars stood tall over the whole of creation and Sūn Wù Kōng scratched his mark upon one of them while laughing his deepest villainous guffaw and stroking the long hairs of his moustache. The monkey leapt back with one mighty spring over the mountains and islands and seas to the open palm of the Lord Buddha, where he pranced and paraded with his chest puffed out, laughing his best villainous cackle while stroking the long hairs of his moustache. *And when are you going to make your jump?* enquired the Lord Buddha, to which Sūn Wù Kōng did a summersault in astonishment and proclaimed that he had already made the jump, and with a single leap had sprung over the mountains and islands and seas to the very edge of the world where the five red pillars stand and there, he had scratched his mark. To which the Lord Buddha showed the monkey his middle finger where the mark of Sūn Wù Kōng was clearly scratched. *All this time,* the Lord Buddha explained, *you have not left my palm.* And so, for losing the contest and for all of the mischief he had made Sūn Wù Kōng was imprisoned on Earth for five hundred years. The ruthless, fiercely loyal members of The Yamaguchi-gumi know they belong to the most powerful Gokudō syndicate, but the saikō-komon of the inner circle understand full well that they operate upon a handkerchief held in the palm of The Hand.

Bob Beagrie

She'd been asked by the editor of a publishing house if she could run a poetry workshop for students at the university where he worked. What was she interested in? he asked, because whatever it was, the students were bound to be interested in that, too. Which made *her* sound interesting and was, frankly, a little flattering, if not downright ingratiating. He was a lecturer in modern literature and had once featured her in an essay with three other women poets, exploring the relationship they had with each other. There was no actual relationship, but he'd found one through their work, even though she'd never read the other women. And, she imagined, not them her. But then everything was possible in a small pond.

He was a man she knew, but not well, even though he'd written that essay and published some of her poems in a journal and once in an anthology. When she emailed her reply, it seemed to take ages to say what it was she was interested in. Feeling her way towards it in ever-longer sentences. For instance, the word for *verses* in poetry is *stanzas* and that comes from the Italian language. The Italian for *room*. So, she knew it was something to do with entering the shapes of poems: squares and rectangles, rooms and frames, ekphrasis, photography, paintings, the act of framing, the verb. Then the act of writing about what is framed. What is included and what is omitted. That kind of thing. And cameras of all kinds, especially *camera obscuras*, she'd said.

In bed that night, reading a novel and sipping water from the glass beside her bed, drawing her feet up inside her nightdress, she had the thought that it should have been *cameras obscura*. She reached for her phone to Google it and found that *camera obscuras* was acceptable, but that *cameras obscurae* was, technically, correct. Then there was the camera lucida, a different thing altogether. That was a small gadget, though related through the ocular. An aid to drawing, highly technical in itself, and difficult to grasp from a verbal description. Whereas the camera obscura was a dark room which had a tiny hole in one wall, sometimes a lens, and that projected an image of the outside world or of people who stood in it onto the back wall.

The image was upside down and left to right. Everything turned on its head. She experienced that once in a museum in Edinburgh with one of her lovers. They sat in the darkness as the door was closed and there was the world turned upside down. For some reason the man had turned to kiss her. Not a man, really, but a boy emerging from his teens, the way the world was emerging into that darkened box. She pushed against his chest, gently. She wasn't ready for that yet, but she was a few days later when she visited his student flat in the city, just a couple of miles from the university. He'd seemed suddenly vulnerable and that had been enough to lead him to his rumpled bed which she had to make before they made love.

What she remembered was a low hum. The camera obscura had a ventilation system and she wondered if that was because somebody might get locked inside. She imagined gasping for air with that image of the city beside her, its spires and tower blocks and traffic moving on the roads. Arthur's seat in the far distance. More like a film than a photograph. Though she knew the first portable cameras – those early pinhole cameras – had been developed from the idea.

What happened to Will, she didn't know. They'd had a brief and unsatisfactory affair for a few weeks. She'd woken one morning convinced that she was pregnant. She couldn't have said exactly why, but it was a feeling that seemed to suffuse her, making her drowsy, as if the spirit world might take her to itself. She believed in that kind of thing in those days. Long-ago days into which William had so artfully disappeared. She had her period soon after, and that was that. In fact, she'd never become pregnant, never had children. Not yet, and very likely not ever. Which suddenly seemed a long time.

So that was her train of thought. Lying in bed, reading a novel about imperial Russia. Thinking of that little spelling error in her email and how it might be received by the academic who'd asked her to do the workshop. *Whatever interests you, really.* Wondering about the students she'd be teaching in just a few weeks' time. How she'd introduce herself. How she'd place the little Rolleiflex camera on the table and pass it round. The baby Rolleiflex, four by four. You couldn't get film for it anymore. Each student would look down at the glass screen inside the metal box that unfolded at the top and recognise the world framed in their hands.

They'd invariably smile at that moment. She wondered where she might take things after that. Putting down her book. Taking a last sip of water. Switching off the light, so that there was a momentary after-image before the dark. All that was something to do with poetry, which she was interested in.

Graham Mort

35MM

The smell of damp earth and burning tyres, a house left abandoned for the endless winter. Matted feathers tumbling down a dirt road. A near-empty bus scuttles across fissures, bumping at the edge of a different time zone. Everything is the colour of stained coffee cups and nicotine; everything feels like an old man's complaining bones. Chickens peck at the ground, as if impatient to break through to anywhere but here. A tree, so bare it's forgotten the implications of leaves, leans on a tottering shelter, wherein sits the love of my life, swathed in muted green and gold. She hasn't smoked for years, but she sparks up a cigarette with her father's lighter. She doesn't drink, but her breath is apple wine as she sings one of her mother's songs. I've never been here before, but it's all familiar from arthouse films; and when the love of my life raises her face in my direction, the bus, the chickens, and the subtle string soundtrack I'd not even noticed up until this point, all fall silent as damp earth.

Oz Hardwick

NIGHT CRIES

In velvet tunnels
the mole's needle incisors
bring punctured ultrasonic screams.

In the lane's canopy
feather rustles branch.
The whiffling owl's knowing screech
curt,
unbelievably impudent
a shout at a sacred ritual.

In the hedge
the fox cub's curdling keen
a baby shrieking
like it could draw blood.

In the ceiling
the cottage creaks,
claws and beaks
scrattle the weatherboard,
chewing and grinding
muck and sawdust.

In my dream
an old friend
sighs and murmurs
like a lover.

Keith Willson

BRIDE OR
BROOM

My best friend,
lover, light
of my life,
significant other,
soon-to-be-wife
may be shocked
to discover
on Saturday nights
when she's out
with her mates
drinking cocktails
till late
that I dance
in my pants
to the theme
to Swan Lake
with the broom
as my date
and the broom
dances great,
sweeps me off
of my feet
till my head's
in a state
but I keep
it a secret
for her sake.

Simon Tindale

Once Upon a Time

The stars are good tonight,
bright in a clear January sky.
The orange-gold lights of the city
are muted by frosty blackness

and you are the astronomer
you wanted to be age ten,
have observed these stars
from *El Roque de Los Muchachos*.

As if a musician with perfect pitch,
know their catalogue numbers,
their light year distances, and
seven spectral classes from M to O,

their life cycles and mechanisms;
the jumps in key as nucleosynthesis
burns hydrogen, then helium,
silicon to nickel in supernova collapse.

You never met your life's love
in a snowstorm at Tooting Bec,
never had four children or learned
how to pronounce *metastasis,*

and so tonight,
your only pain is the long grief
of cosmological death.

Ruth Aylett

THE RETURN

when the dead return
they dust themselves down
look around as if trying to explain
how they could have tripped
and fallen
they fit limbs back to torso
adjust the hole in their head
put their face on again
go back to inspect
their home
search among the rubble
for things they remember
a child's ball
framed photos
a mobile phone
they try to fit their key into the lock
in a door that no longer exists
where the threshold
opens onto a gaping hole
and the sky and stars look down
without a sigh
and the wind whispers
but says nothing
nothing

Colin Pink

Today I saw the ghost of myself,
he was standing on the shore
preoccupied with something – there but not there.
We both knew things were about to get worse.
I called out, told him that he should talk,
but my words were lost in the constant
murmur of waves nudging at the sand.

Today I met the ghost of myself,
he'd carried his weight through time.
I tried to tell him to put it down
or it would drag us both under,
but drowning men are always
far too busy to shout
and what do I know, I'd made those same mistakes.

Today I watched the ghost of myself,
he followed me from the beach,
his old Mitsubishi in the rear-view mirror.
I tried flashing my lights
to warn him of the road ahead,
but he didn't seem to notice
as he drove past with hardly a glance.

Today I found the ghost of myself,
he was sat in the corner
with that look, was it sympathy or fear,
as if he knew all the roads
I still had to travel.
I tried to tell him he should leave me alone
but my words were always wasted on him.

Kemal Houghton

THE SMALL PRINT

With a golden thread, to stitch
Ourselves the angel wings we imagine
We deserve, there or thereabouts – but before
The glory pose, the small print

The Kingdom of Jesus says first
We have to die – heartbeat faint as footfall
Of a saint, to seraphim with dented trumpets
The death-rattle and *shazam*

In the old poems, tales of true love
Ended at a gallows, or with tender flesh
And burning brands – now, robots rack
Our salad days, thinning weaker stems

Life is difficult, love's quantum declarations
In slipknot arrays of here and now, charged
Particles spoiling our languid afternoons – our
Table talk as mismatched as the cutlery

This elegy is ours, the image recognised
Too late as *other* – some dapper rogue, acid
Innuendos amusing in their time, now herald
Of a cold regime, friendless on a ghostly plane

Estill Pollock

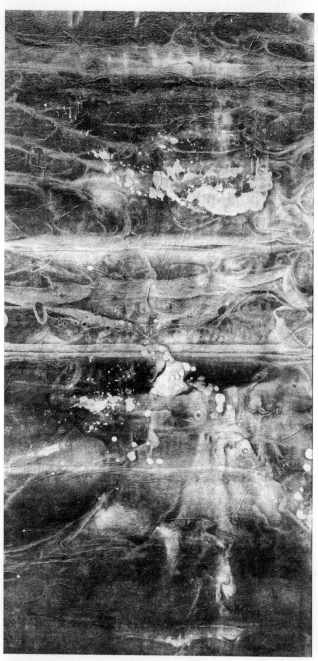

Cosmic Ocean

As at your graveside we, your mourners, weep
From over where the rude forefathers lie
I hear a chuntering. They're muttering in their sleep.
Is it in welcome that they softly sigh?

You must be joking. Welcome? Not from them.
They're making sure you know you trespass here.
"Bloody incomers," is the requiem
They sing for you. They'd like to make it clear

You are not one of them, and though you've spent
A quarter of a century or more
In this stone-faced village, they still resent
Your presence here. Nor will your death ensure

You're finally accepted. Not a bit
Of it. It will not change a blessed thing
Befriended by your neighbours? Far from it.
You'll be cold-shouldered while you're mouldering.

Not one of them will pass the time of day.
Like the quick, they'll keep themselves to themselves.
They'll not relent now you have passed away
But lie, tight-lipped and silent, in their graves.

George Jowett

LOOP

Embalmed in cedar oil, trophy heads
Strung from the necks of horses – Celt warriors beyond
The gates taunting
Roman garrisons far from Spain or Gaul

Centurions along the wall, stamping
Their feet against the cold, watching the riders
Pass and turn, pass and turn, always
Just out of arrowshot

In the Spring, cohorts crossed the narrow sea
Then traced the land's spine north, and now
Hard duty here, this stain of tundra
And guttural guile

Agricola sent orders – attack-dog legions
Rome's realpolitic against the dark, no
Notion of muddy stalemate or the rumbling bellies
Of wind-chilled sentries

Among the wildlings, women
Rough as the painted horses – one bares
Her ass, strutting in the captain's helmet, its red plume
Wafting like a dare
…

The Viking hulk burning on the tide

The skin of the corpse a yellowed milk evaporating
In the flames – the sword and harness, green
Jewels inlaid in pockets
Of filigree gold, the day failing, shunted
Into shadows

The priest's face smeared with ash, and across
His eyes a thumb streak of madder, the altar
Stinking of sanctified blood – but the gods
Are elsewhere

Here, petty feuds
Mimicking mouths of dark alleys – spent treaties
Burning to the waterline

In oily lamplight, old lies, ground
To an edge – parley's cold blade, the child-bride
The penance and the prize
…

I sink into prehistory landscapes, dreams
Surging at Play Station velocity

A stone flicked nimbly shattered
The Elizabethan pane – my wilder days
Behind me, tethered to iambics now

Birnam Wood a palm oil plantation – before
Those tetchy thanes brokered
North Sea drilling futures, witches glimpsed
A crown, thistles bound in compass points of blood

Long memory exacts a toll – a Celtic knot
Carved into a funeral stone

The dead king's signature on the affidavit, the last page
Bursting into flames, statecraft repeating
The lies of others

In the distance, breath, ghostly in the cold, punctuates
Positions of archers along the wall

Estill Pollock

DEATH HANGS AROUND

in school playgrounds,
sneaks away the odd child.

We watched Anne die, aged nine;
drugs bloated her face to a full moon.

They may have spoken of her death
afterwards; I don't remember.

In the 1950s, grown-ups whispered,
least said, soonest mended.

Tonnie Richmond

INHERITANCE
*(In 19th century Britain the names of deceased infants were often
re-used for their siblings)*

You grieve each short-lived child –
  what's in a name: quickening, gathering

mourned, hearts torn, stones
  engraved the same; babies by the bushel

given names still warm from siblings
  mourned, the christening gown hardly worn –

the epitaph's refrain repeats the same
    bereaved and borrowed name.

Anne Eyries

ALL ACTION HERO

He looks up with a smile wide as a rainbow
goes from nought to sixty in five seconds
eyes flick to doubt, lips curl in existential
pain, body shudders, convulses, writhes.
Screams pummel me; punch drunk
I walk him on trochaic lines.

All forgotten, head heavy on my arm
I lean over into his crib, one hoody cord
falls, dangling millimetres from his face
like Tom Cruise in Mission Impossible
suspended above the alarmed floor.

His back touches down on the mattress
and I am Indiana Jones switching
golden idol for a bag of sand
sliding my hand from under him
praying his sapphire eyes stay closed
that no darts shoot from his mouth.

Bars on all four sides cannot hold him.
He raises one arm straight above his head
shows me how to fly.

David Thompson

I take you for a spin past the sink
extractor hood and oven, circle
the dining table and chairs, form
a figure of eight, the breakfast bar
the fulcrum, its hourglass shape
of sweeping bends and tight turns
suggests the time ticking as I mark
laps against the cooker clock
racing you to those pit stops:
crying ceased, eyes closed,
legs flopped, settled enough
to lay in your cot. I worry
about losing grip, that I might
leave the track, hit the barriers
if I stray from the racing line.

David Thompson

MIDNIGHT PACING

I walk you back and forth at night,
try to rock, sway, bump you to sleep
count my slow bobbing laps
will your eyes to close
on the tenth, fifteenth, twentieth …

I hold my urine as if to teach you.
The blanket slips off when you kick
I retrieve it each time, play pretend
that I can provide you the warmth
of the crib by your mother's side.

Halfway across the landing, the LED
from the fire alarm spotlights your face.
We're meant to protect this household
but when called upon, all we can do
is let out a panicked screech.

David Thompson

When I was ten, I recall a nebulous feeling, a craving, for something missing. It was hearing fragments of pop music on the radio intertwined with the hiss of presses in my father's dry-cleaning plant. It was the tinny tunes like "Downtown" played over and over on the tabletop jukeboxes at Gus's diner. It was the silence in our house on long summer days when Mom retreated to her bedroom for indeterminate hours – and the TV wouldn't do. Wouldn't keep me company. The little transistor radio I got for a birthday did not seem to do the trick.

I discovered a box of ancient 78 records Dad picked up at an auction. A few of these heavily scratched artifacts, last played on a crank Victrola, were my first encounter with classical music. A symphony by Edvard Grieg was my favorite of the lot, but it didn't hit quite right. It was closer, though. I played these old records on a stereo which I thought for the longest time was just another piece of furniture as I had never heard any sound from it. It would have been nice to hear some tunes and watch my parents jitterbug around the room. Maybe everything would have been a bit different in our house with music and dancing. There was a large potted plant on the lid which was inconvenient to move at each use, and I found a few odd but somewhat more contemporary records in the cabinet beneath the phonograph: the Ink Spots, a typical, early rock and roll group of the '50s from the era of Buddy Holly, and *Songs from the Red Army Choir*. (I wondered if Dad was secretly a communist and I should report this to the FBI.) I learned how to operate the gismo and was astonished that it worked and at the quality of the sound. Mom bought my first record, Sonny and Cher's *In Case You're in Love*. I wasn't quite sure what to do while listening to it, how many times I should listen to the songs, or how enthusiastic I should be about the experience. Somehow, I missed all the great music of the '60s.

Dad bought a player piano around this time. It was of a dark brown cracked varnish, hideously out of tune. Its motor was an old vacuum cleaner and drowned out the music which was mostly plunky ragtime or quaint tunes from the '20s and '30s. But it was entertaining to feed the yellowed brittle rolls into the machine and watch the keys rise and fall on their own accord in synchronization with holes in the script. Mom talked about piano lessons for my sister or herself, but this did not materialize. The top of the piano became the location for the new 8-track stereo. Dad played easy listening like Perry Como or Herb Alpert while he worked on the payroll, the adding machine providing a rude percussion accompaniment. We left the piano where it was when we were forced to move when Dad lost the house and cleaners.

In fifth grade, much to the dismay of the ears of Grandpa's dog Henry, I picked up the trumpet. For four years, we were all tortured with band favorites like "Red River Valley," "It's a Grand Old Flag" and "The King and I". Henry howled, more vocal than anyone, begging for the clamor to stop. The gift of a book of show tunes provided no alleviation for anyone. The asinine pointlessness of marching band encouraged me to finally say "enough is enough." My sister experimented with band and trumpet for a year or two. When I momentarily considered picking it up again, I found the bell smashed, crumpled like a car fender and the valves seized pistons.

Just before Mom's paranoia surfaced, when we were still all mostly happy at home, she bought a new violin for Dad at Christmas. At the time, we were still reluctant to view this as rather crazy. Dad did not read music and never played another instrument. He sang a bit for community theatre musicals like *Guys and Dolls*, but that was the extent of his talent and interest in music. And, why a violin? Dad was more preoccupied with hunting and antique car restoration. The image of Dad as violinist or even fiddle player did not fit. It appeared as an awkward means of civilizing Dad and our home. The puzzled look on Dad's face on Christmas morning was telling. He never attempted to play it. I used it more as a still-life prop in creating Picasso-like cubist paintings.

I had an 8-track player hanging beneath the dash of my first car. Installed it myself. But the songs it played were for my friends and girls on first dates. In art class, Mr. Boddy played one of three records depending upon his mood that day: Boston's *Don't Look Back*, something by Steely Dan, and Bach's *Sonatas for Cello and Piano*. Maybe the Bach. Finally, something began to resonate. Close, but not quite. From there I discovered a deluge of composers, and I was nearly certain it was Mozart's sonatas and piano concertos which conversed with my heart and head. It was Chopin, finally Chopin. Finally, I could make some sense of the world through Waltzes, Etudes, Mazurkas, Ballads, Preludes and Nocturnes. For the first time I thought, with this beauty in my ears, I might be able to navigate the noise of the world.

David Sapp

FATHER AT 6 A.M.

Before his wife wakes to her teaching load
before the children grumble out of bed
before the traffic the office
before meetings memos knocking heads together
before the day gets going –
a tour of the house
drawing curtains raising blinds
letting the cat out or in
then setting the breakfast table
with tablecloth napkins toast rack
cereal bowls plates knives spoons
muesli cornflakes orange juice milk
marmalade Vegemite jam.
The radio is a quiet prayer.
Now the kettle now tea
now he calls *Time to get up!*
Time to get up!
all through the house.

Hilaire

He has always been a good dad.

#

Jack in a box, the world of Jack; with his son sitting beside him the car feels like a different space. Most Saturday lunchtimes Malcolm picks Jack up from home. As he steps into the house Jack is raring to go, dragging the fleece and scarf off its hook, worrying they'll be late for the match, spurning goodbyes, slipping into the front seat of the Jag.

#

"He is faking it, Jack. There's no blood."

"Get him off!" Jack leans forward.

Their team is heading for relegation.

This is nirvana for Malcolm, being in the moment. He's connected with Jack; he is contained. There are clear lines here where the vital things go on: the penalty box, the six-yard box, the eighteen-yard box. This is the way to live your life. Step outside, you don't win. *Map out your future*, his mantra to his students, know which boxes you fit in.

At half-time Malcolm remains in his seat, head cupped in hands, the sun on his balding head. An away game, far enough from home. This week's match is Premier League, big, and easy for Malcolm and Jack to get lost in the crowd. Still, he lets Jack go off, away from him, just to be sure.

"Get me a burger too, son, OK?"

Jack walks off shoulders slumped. Three-nil without a hope of scoring.

"Malcolm Reid isn't it?" A shout from two rows down.

Malcolm pulls on his flat tweed cap over his forehead, stands his jacket collar up as if to hide from a sharp wind, ignoring the calm spring sunshine. Malcolm imagines his heart visible, bleeding at his feet. Eyes lit up in happy recognition, grey at the sides and temple, Bob Wilson, years older but still familiar as his pal, one of the gang he used to hang around with in the before-children days.

"We must catch up!" Bob is twisted in his seat. Will he try to push past up to Malcolm's row?

From insomniac forebodings to reality. He stands up, concocts an urgent face, saying "Must go... See you another time …" He doesn't look back.

They are stuck getting out of the car park at the ground, impatient drivers braking and tooting as if riding the dodgems.

#

Malcolm is a good dad, listens to his son. "We did the slave trade this week, Dad. It was bad wasn't it?" Jack growing more alert to a wider world. Starting to question his own place in the world? Does Jack ask his mother questions about Malcolm's place in his life?

"So-o-o … how did the English project go at school?"

"Yeah."

"And it was about …?" Has Jack, at only twelve years old, reached the I'm-a-teenager-and-only-grunt stage since last week?

"Dad, that was last month! We're doing *The Tempest* now."

"Of course, of course. Is it good?"

"I like the bit at the beginning where they nearly drown." Malcolm remembers the sloshing and knocking around of the shipwreck scene he watched in an amateur production years ago. He had been tempted to laugh out loud, in a mixture of embarrassment and unease, neither voiced to the girlfriend who sat holding his hand.

"Dad, it's parents' evening on Monday."

"Yes I know." Malcom's clipped reply an attempt to convince himself. "I'll try and make it but … we've been through this before Jack, it's a long way to come and what with work …"

"You've never been."

"You hungry? There's the chippie."

No more paper wrappings, soggy chips. Malcolm holds back a contented sigh as he watches the battered fish slipping neatly into the lidded box, alongside a carefully placed shovel of chips. Tidy cups of peas, lids clicked automatically into place placed in a boxy paper carrier, a large cartoon-ish blue fish on the side.

"This is nice isn't it, son?" Embraced by the front seats of the Jag, Malcolm and Jack eat silently. Malcolm would be happy to linger in the small space, a gift box.

The background rumble of the motorway lulls the soft body of his son, half-lying on the front seat. The stodgy meal and the match loss hang heavy with them both. Malcolm glances over and for an instant is loose-moored and frail.

Back on the doorstep Dawn kisses both Jack and Malcolm. After all these years it is a kind of marriage. Malcolm had told her, honestly, that first time after meeting in the pub, that this would be an open relationship. No commitment. Then, somehow he had been drawn in to a Saturday arrangement once he knew about Jack. He couldn't help himself when Jack wanted to support his team.

Dawn had eventually settled down. She didn't yell like a fishwife any more, demand *He needs a dad, a proper dad.* Her temper used to arouse him. She would give in. But he'd stay away from her for weeks. Then, usually, he'd stay over. She's kept herself a sexy girl. He's insisted there'd be no more pregnancies. He gave her a generous cash allowance, no danger of her going to the Child Support Agency, he'd too much to lose. She was allowed to give Jack the surname, Robinson. That's him, Malcolm *Robinson*. Cautious with her from the start.

#

This Saturday Malcolm swings his legs out of bed. The black and yellow circled wallpaper is an affront to his sense of taste. It only feeds his resentment at his 'situation' so he turns away from that one wall at every opportunity. Shivering, he reaches to the chair for his thick, red dressing gown. He's still not used to putting money in a meter.

He does not want this day on him. Out of habit his clothes are tidy. On one of the yet-to-be-unpacked boxes he roots around in a jacket pocket for his wallet. Thank god the card is in his name. He's found the corner shop, there'll be something he can get for his tea.

Weekends are not real. Over and over Malcolm replays recent events when he cannot distract himself with Netflix, or funding matters he must attend to as head of department. Perhaps he should get a dog to replace Elsa? People are not the only ones he misses.

He would have to do the cleaning up himself, regularly, after a dog. The flat is tiny. Cracks in the ambiguously grey kitchen floor are filled with beads of a darker shade unnoticed by the estate agent's inventory. The large windows would bring light if only a window cleaner came to scrape off bird droppings and grit. A dog wouldn't mind.

If he did seek advice he knows it would be *take one day at a time*. Bloody therapy, you can't avoid hearing it talked about on the TV, the women at work. Sunday tomorrow. He conjures all the Sundays up like an old film he cannot help watching: *Always in time for lunch he would slide into the sweeping driveway of the gracious stone-built suburban house, press the button beside him for the electric window to swish right down, greeting him with the rich smell of new mown grass. The gardening company would have been with their sit-on mower, neatening the edges of back and front lawns. Nat'd be pleased.*

Walking across to the heavy wooden front door, past the basketball net on the side wall. Inside the roomy hall no one about.

"Nat, I'm home!"

"Daddy, daddy!" Lucy, his 11-year old, rushes up to him. "You were drunk again last night weren't you. Naughty Daddy!"

Ben, his 14-year old son, inclined to resent Malcolm's weekend absences, would stay holed up for an hour or two before emerging from his bedroom.

Nat emerges from the kitchen, greeting him lightly with a cheek kiss, mock-frowning. "And was Derek in his cups too?" She'd use these old-fashioned expressions as a genial wifely chiding.

That final Sunday spilled out as a heavy silence as he'd closed the front door behind him. A disordered stack of cardboard cartons, and anarchic heaps of his clothes blockaded the hall. Someone who looked like Nat but with pale face and black shadows under her eyes brandished her arm in dismissal: *Those are yours to take.* He held up both palms, a fortress of feigned ignorance.

"Bumped into Bob Wilson, he's moved near here." Next to the newel post, Nat with arms folded, a shield. "Funny you have a son who goes to football matches with you."

" What's he…

"… looked all very homely he said."
An upsurge of bitterness raged; the children sheltering upstairs.

#

He sits at the square plastic table picking at the chicken curry-and-rice ready-meal. The black and yellow circles in the wall are fading, traded for a ghostly, pale-brown surface. The other three walls and the alcove where his single bed sits, have already turned to cardboard, the corner displaying staples, a large sticker on one, FRAGILE in bright red capitals. He looks up – the artexed ceiling has disappeared. In its place four precisely overlapping light brown flaps.

Moira Garland

There's something I've been meaning to talk to you about for some time now, it's kind of delicate, and I can't figure out a way to do it gently, so I'm going to just dive right in, I hope you won't mind, I really do.

It started out when I took a flight to Berlin a month or so ago. I boarded the plane, stowed my bag and settled down quickly, minding my own business as usual. Although I hadn't acknowledged her to that point, I became increasingly aware of the female passenger beside me fluttering and fussing around her seat, with her bags, with her coat, her various accoutrements for the flight, so much so that I turned to help her just to put an end to the drama, for the sake of everyone on board. Then I get stunned by a moment of recognition, it's a fraction of a second, our eyes engaged in furious communication. Hers were deep sea blue, probably lenses, the faintest of smiles and a hint of patronage. She was older than me, I guessed around your age, swept back silver hair, cosmetically precise, sharp and purposefully dressed in white trouser suit.

"Can I help you with that? Here let me lift the bag."

"No, it's fine, thank you but it's not heavy." Her voice was laced with a smoky quality, she was watching me the whole time. I registered something in her manner, her deportment, unknowable to both of us at first, a subtle stirring of familiarity. Once airborne I couldn't quite shake off the intrigue. I began to suspect she was deliberately ignoring me, unnaturally cool, so when flight service came, I turned to face her and said something about airline food and the drinks never having enough ice. It opened a door, I gently stepped through.

"Do you like Berlin?"

"Yes, I've been going every year for a while, visiting my son, my stepson."

Something about the cadence of her voice sounded familiar, like a groove from the past, I thought perhaps from our side of London, where we lived while Dad was working in Asia. She asked if I was travelling for business, I explained about the family company, how we fly around Europe looking for suppliers. At this juncture she becomes more animated, asking questions, leaning into me intently as we talked. After a while I need a break from the interrogation and redirect.

"So, are you from North London originally?"

"What makes you think North?"

"Oh, you know, they say those born and bred one side of the river can tell the difference."

"Barnet, actually."

"Oh, that's interesting, my father started a factory in Enfield back in the sixties.

"Yes, I know." She seemed to speak these words from an unmeasurable distance, I leant forward for clarification.

"Sorry?"

"...I knew your father." A slight pause pre-empted the bomb, a split second of integrity. But do you know what? She couldn't help herself, she had to say it, had to let the thing out of the bottle, the allure and the drama proved ineluctable.

"What? How? Do you know who I am?... Did you know... when you saw me? How did you know my father? The business?" I rattled off the questions, incredulous; she smiled reservedly. I have to tell you that at this moment the whole situation seemed slightly absurd, I thought maybe the drinks, the altitude had something to do with it. Who exactly was this woman sitting next to me on this flight? She tried to tell me that I looked like my father, that she recognised me in him, she told me that she worked at the plant in the sixties, as a line worker in the factory, she would have been barely eighteen.

"But you said you knew him? How well did a young girl working on the factory line know the owner of the factory?"

Now I need to make a declaration, I'm a firm believer in probabilities. Coincidence doesn't exist, just greater or lesser chances of something happening, statistics and chaos is all there is. I sensed randomness being overhauled by a creeping realisation. I have memories of Dad being away in Asia much of the time when I was small. This woman said she saw him walking the factory floor, and that he occasionally stopped to talk to the workers, that he was a very charismatic man, everybody loved him. He gave presents to his favourite workers at Christmas. I tried an oblique question.

"I remember him being away a lot, have *you* ever travelled to the Far East?" This was the one that took the lid off the box, I could tell I had unhinged her, and I suddenly realised we hadn't even exchanged names. I lowered my voice for some reason, conscious that I might be about to reveal something painfully delicate to the whole aircraft, despite the droning engine noise.

"Do you know my name?" She tucked her chin deep into her neck and looked up at me with contrition, her voice fluttering with emotion.

"Yes, I do, ... Michael. Dear Michael."

OK look, I'm going to cut to the chase now, get this whole thing out into the open. I just wanted you to understand how completely insane this whole experience was for me, how incredibly uncomfortable the whole reveal was, and how conflicted I felt when I heard the truth ... yes, the truth, about me.

We got off the flight, worked our way through customs and baggage claim, and I had time enough to take her to a coffee shop in the airport so that she could fill in the back story. She had set the whole thing up. I think she just wanted to reach out to her real son, her only son, apparently conceived on a business trip to Tokyo, and let him know of her existence. The separation had finally become too much for her to bear. In the beginning she had coped, always received information about my life, my achievements, took pride from a distance. But as she grew older the temptation to contact me while she still had time had become an unbearably heavy load. Eventually she found a way to track my movements and befriend someone at the company who managed to get the details of my flight from a colleague, even the seat allocation once my secretary had checked me in. As I left her and walked towards the taxi rank, I felt unsteady on my legs, it seemed my knees would hinge and collapse at any moment. The shock was complete, but her story had a ring of truth, I believed it.

So you see, dear mother, I don't know if it was ever your intention to tell me, in the past or any time in the future, but I just wanted you to know that it really doesn't matter. This doesn't change a thing. Whatever motivations, whatever pressures came to bear, nothing alters the fact that I think of you as my real mother. How could this ever be otherwise, after all that we've been through together? After every minute you've cared for me, every bump and bruise lovingly soothed, all those evenings you fought off sleep until you heard my key in the door? We are made of tiny bundles of DNA, genes are immutable and passed down generations, but our emotions are forged in an unquenchable fire, and this is where my love for you resides, forever burnished and bright as the sun.

Steve Smith

When I was not quite old enough to stay home alone, I sat in the car in the vast parking lot waiting for Mom to finish her shopping in Big Bear Supermarket. Bored, bored, bored, I calculated I spent half of my childhood waiting for Mom. And sometimes, without any advance notice, we'd stop at her mother's for another hour or more on the way home. Never mind the meat or frozen foods. There was absolutely nothing to do at Grandma Dearman's tiny sad house on Lawn Avenue. The yard was nominal and threadbare. I was not allowed to explore the garage as it leaned like a swayback horse ready to fall in upon Grandpa's two-tone red and white 1957 Chevy Bel Air with the stylish tail fins. It sat immobilized, its tires rotting in the dirt floor.

There was never any forethought as to bringing something to keep me occupied like books, my little Matchbox cars, or a bag of plastic army men to wage battles in the grass. I knew in the attic there was a saber in its scabbard, as long as I was tall, that belonged to a Confederate Civil War relative, but I was not permitted to play with it – only know that it was there and not to be touched. The kids across the street were not allowed to play with me or I was not allowed to mix with them. I wasn't sure which, and there was no explanation. We eyed one another from opposite sidewalks, a wide river or demilitarized zone between us, and considered the risk for new playmates. When the boredom became overwhelming, the sight of their bikes and toys was a torture. On nice summer days, as a last resort, I excavated small roads in the dirt and erected flimsy houses of twigs and leaves surrounded by pebbles. But even at that age, I knew this to be a pathetic substitute and begged to go home.

The ordeal worsened when it rained or was too cold to go out. I was required to sit quietly on the davenport of the cramped living room. There was no TV. Grandpa Dearman filled much of the room, an old farmer now reduced to spending his days sitting in a hard wooden rocker with a cane in his lap and a brass tobacco spittoon at his side. I recall only one occasion when he spoke to me, and it was a frightening one-sided conversation. The gist of his discourse was he found children unpleasant and should be "seen and not heard." He gripped the cane tightly when he spoke. Grandma, usually in the kitchen, could only be reached by passing close by the ogre and his foul-smelling pot. I could sense it then, but I later confirmed that my mother hated her father, and the feeling was mutual. There was a family rumor that Lewis Dearman was ordered by the court to never discipline his children. So, why these visits?

On the wall across from the sofa were the only two pictures in the house. One was of Jesus, the popular 1940 Warner Sallman version. It was the soft, gauzy portrait, a long-haired Jesus looking into a vague distance. I thought it was odd that Jesus with long hair was acceptable, but "dirty, long-haired hippies" protesting the Vietnam War were an abomination. It was certainly not the Catholic version where Jesus is looking straight at you while holding the Sacred Heart. This was a very protestant Jesus. As staunch Baptists, there was suspicion of Catholics in this family and resentment when my mother married one. Jesus' constant gaze was directed toward Grandpa's permanent locale – perhaps my grandmother's attempt to somehow soften him or at least keep his rage at bay. Though not a source of contemplation, Jesus was suitable to look upon, I suppose, but he seemed disinterested in my plight.

The other picture was a landscape of mountains, a cheap reproduction on pressed printed paper. My other set of grandparents, Dad's family, owned a nearly identical version hanging above their television, and we displayed a variation above our fireplace mantel. The original was probably an equally cheap production oil painting, mass-produced for big hotel sales advertised late at night for "this-weekend-only." Each year at the Knox County Fair, an artist would display similar overly palatable scenes in his trailer booth. I relished watching him paint on plates and canvases more than reviewing the livestock, riding the Scrambler, or attending the demolition derby. Grandma's masterpiece was a typical view of pure wilderness, craggy peaks, misted over at the top and overlooking a pleasant meadow. A shaft of yellow light illuminated the center of the view, and there was no trace of any human presence. Affixed to the couch in that tiny room, there was nothing else that provided any other stimulus or refuge but, try as I might, I could not imagine myself in the painting. There was no escape for me there, and the picture was as trapped as I.

When I studied art history in college, I became acquainted with Albert Bierstadt's romanticized American landscapes. And while at a conference in Colorado, I trekked to Estes Park and experienced first-hand Bierstadt's exhilarating view of the Rocky Mountains. I'm fairly certain that I stood in the very spot where the artist planted his easel. There were many people in the park admiring the same view. I thought that they, like me, were all from Ohio and had similar inadequate paintings above their mantels, televisions, and couches – that this was their pilgrimage to reconcile the bad art of their childhoods with the splendor of reality. And I wondered if there were an equal number of visitors to Ohio from Colorado who had horrendous paintings of idealized cornfields in their homes and were at that moment visiting an Ohio cornfield to appreciate the actual scene.

David Sapp

Thomas Writes His Sister's Name

Elbows bent, feet together, legs outstretched,
speechless as an island on the sea-blue waves
of the classroom floor in his green hard-hat,
Thomas aged ten, sits and writes his sister's name.

Presenting piece by vivid wooden piece,
hovering at the frame like finger-tips on braille,
he scans from left to right, and right to left.
One by one, sense perception and elimination

get the sequence right and slot her letters home.
Each successful placement swings his arms
and drums his heels. And when her name's

complete, CATHERINE writ large,
Thomas spills his sister overboard
and starts to write her name again

Phil Connolly

THOMAS AND THE BIRTHDAY STONES

Teetering on shingle in his red hard-hat
and brand-new *Nike* socks and trainers,
well-wrapped up for winter, shaking off

his gloves as fast as dad can fit them on,
Thomas quivers like a dowser's rod, readies
himself but checks, to our surprise, his aim –

mum's plea to miss the mallards thinking bread.
An hour trips past; stones committed
to the Lune turn his throwing hand blue.

Dad suspects he wants them back,
the way his famous namesake chuffs
into the dark, goes AWOL for a while

then whistles, beams and billows out
to greet the light and Thomas, all
anticipation at the tunnel's mouth.

But like the letters Postman Pat pushes
through Greendale's doors, the stones are gone;
the river swallows them for good.

Bone cold, we're keen to call a halt,
head for the warmth of home, or find a pub.
But this is Thomas's fourteenth birthday treat;

he's deep into the stones and can't stop.
So it's more of the same: we comb the bank
for size and shape, fix them in his grip,

then stand hard by and watch: a wobbly lob,
the blink it takes a stone to sink
from sunless splash to clunk on rocks.

Phil Connolly

Dawn Unfolding

JONATHAN ARTHUR

Long before sunrise, Arthur is running
up and down the hall: soft slipper-thumps.
He dresses up in black NHS frames, no lenses,
to celebrate dawn with brekkie and numbers:
how many Weetabix in the box, in his bowl.
Arthur's pyjamas are printed with maps –
his nights swift, he dreams over nameless lands,
sweeps oceans, but in daylight he cannot
travel far alone. After swigs of milk,
he scoots into her room, clambers onto the bed
and gently pulls back her eyelids. They open;
they shut tight. He tests again. She groans.
He billows his sister a breeze with the duvet,
tries to shock her awake – look, a giant caterpillar
on the carpet. Silent – she who gathers words
to share with him: 'buffet', 'luncheon', 'frontier'.
He pours a spillage of chatter over her, to launch
their journey. *Annie, Annie! I'm ready!*

*

It's late, late. Three hundred miles apart,
we speak on screen. I note the puffiness of face,
the purplish tinge to his eyelids after a spell
of nocturnal number-crunching; his glass of whisky.
Our conversation always begins with food,
as if this were a midnight feast. 'Langres':
texture between fudgy and chalky, a wrinkly
brandy-washed rind; known as 'brain cheese'.
We retreat to the stream of light in a basilica
where it's calmer, but we can never resist lingo –
what are 'brother' and 'sister' in the Latin families?
Fratello and *sorella*, *irmão* and *irmã*.
How to pronounce the endings – is 'slipperier'
grammatical? We replenish our word-house often.
Tangible as Jonny's arm round my shoulder.
My brother's voice is slowing down to drowsy,
untethered, as I am after a blowy run on the shore.
Why say this now. *I'm afraid.*

Anne Ryland

iPad *fired up*, Mum is on the phone
to technical support, my son, Jack.
The search bar has disappeared but
there's a long, grey floating sausage.
Jack rolls his eyes. Her laugh echoes
on both devices but the screen is black.
With each button, she expects an explosion.
Suddenly, as if by witchcraft, she's there,
smiling and young. *Zoom*, she says,
like a child touching the sky on the swings.
She's put on a summer blouse especially.
When she knocks over her wine, everything
capsizes to crackling. Kitchen roll later,
Mum is back. We watch her forehead,
listening to how she thought she'd lost
all of the newts over winter, until
one little swimmer, deep in the depths,
wriggled up to kiss the air.

Stuart Pickford

In Sheltered Accommodation

She sweeps Autumn
From the step,
Leaf after amber leaf.

What matter if the hoover
Stays disconnected?
And the washing-up
Coagulates in the sink?

Summer is a scent
Of geraniums
In the memory
Of yesterday's gossip.

The phone rings,
The doorbell buzzes;
She stares ahead,
Clinically detached
From reason.

On the television,
Nursery rhymes
For mother-and-toddler:

She starts to sing.

Michael Newman

LEEDS BUS STATION

We sit in the queue beside a gateway.
An elderly couple approach,
walking slowly, a man supporting
a woman on his arm. They settle beside us.
He smells unwashed; she is bent
and wasted, her face translucent.
She says they have been to St James's,
heading now for Malton.

Her worn grey eyes look out
past the glass portal, see her mother
waving her off to school at the stop
in Station Road, her little brother too,
cap sideways, socks already slipping;
and the bus she and Wilfred caught
to Scarborough after the wedding.
Behind is the one he stepped off
when he came back from the Falklands,
swept John from her arms and whirled him
round their heads before they put him
onto the 62 from the end of the Avenue,
which stopped at Drummond School,
then the University and went on to Australia.

Home, she adds, prolonging the vowel,
and in the air between us the word changes
to *love, safety, finality.*

William Coniston

BLACKTHORN STICK

Upside down an ersatz golf club
for kids aping the old,
we spoke in golfing tones
to sound like plus-foured folk.

Dad had bought it in his thirties;
though then he had no need.
He mimicked country gentleman
tipped his cap to all he met.

He'd go for walks on Sundays
swinging his stick as walkers do,
rhythmically back and forth,
gnarled root snugly in his fist.

No one now plays golf with it.
In his eighties, Dad still walks.
But leaves his blackthorn stick behind,
says it makes him feel old.

Simon Haines

COMMITTED

You deem it offensive
for me to use this word
when describing a carer
who checks into a room
far away from home
after buying stationery
visiting a pharmacy
then writes a letter
more practical than emotional
to each devastated patient
explaining why she desperately
desperately needs some sleep
and YOU don't think that's
commitment?

Simon Tindale

I put my fingers through the railings, strain my ears to hear their voices through the shuttered windows recalling how the green painted walls, absorbing shouts and screaming smells, tasted of smoke and disinfectant; and how he walked mile after mile on the chequerboard tiles without stepping on the lines, reciting names of football stars, and how they saw her curled up body rocking, softly singing lullabies, longing for the comfort of her mother who could tell her all is well; and how endless sloppy meals and sloppy tea rolled like tears down sloppy clothes onto shoes with broken heels; and how the nights were peppered with bad dreams interspersed with random screams followed by the sound of jangling keys; and how the trolley stood parked in the middle, fully loaded, always at the ready to quell the insurrections; and how they swam in the pool of woolly-headedness drowning in the humdrumness of their incarceration.

Margaret Poynor-Clark

The sanatorium, when it was built in 1924, had only two floors and was an inconspicuous speck on the winding coastline, resembling a pencil eraser or a block of nougat. Since then, floors had been added to it like a monstrous game of jenga and one hundred storeys up, one hundred years later, Countess Fabulosa leaned from the window with her chin in her hands beside a cracked vase of camellias. She watched the ocean. Meanwhile, a frazzled nurse with tired eyes bustled around, humming a tune. The nurse pulled the window shut and ushered Countess Fabulosa back to bed. If she did not rest, Nurse Nelson warned, she would not get better.

It was both late and early. No sign of the freighters and cruise ships and hovercrafts that traversed the patch of sanatorium sea – only the sighing ocean could be heard outside. That made Nurse Nelson think it must be the dead of night, and she was right. But it was early, too. By the clock on the wall in the sanatorium hallway she still had hours until the end of her shift.

"I think we've got mice," Nurse Nelson reported to her colleague as they took a midnight tea break.

"Again?" her colleague repeated, aghast.

"Think I saw some on the fifteenth floor," Nurse Nelson said, stirring her tea absently and looking at nothing.

"I'll get the cat," the colleague said, jumping up.

Nurse Nelson followed her down the corridor, laughing. "Wait, wait – we tried that, remember – that's how we got fleas …"

They rushed through the sanatorium hatching plans to save the building, and it was nice, they thought, to have something to interrupt the monotony of the night shift. So engrossed were they in their discussions, though, that they did not see Countess Fabulosa shuffling into the lifts in her standard-issue dressing gown and then leaving the building. The doorman, a birdlike and vigilant man, had three group chats on his phone and they had all become active at once. He was a lost cause, and Countess Fabulosa was free.

Despite her illness (a terrible case of influenza, which left Count Fabulo so concerned that he paused the round-the-world tour of their boat, the *Merry Celeste,* and deposited Fabulosa at the nearest shoreline hospital) and despite the cruel aching in her bones, Countess Fabulosa slipped down the sanatorium steps and made it to the seafront. It was cold, and quiet, and the sky was a startled orange. She was not alone, though. She saw a few small fires dotted along the beach, and people clustered around them chatting, and there was music from the karaoke man on the pier celebrating "fri-yay night". Countess Fabulosa walked along the sandy and narrow beach, and then headed for the rockpools, which lay beyond the pier. It was at these rockpools that he waited for her.

His skin was like clay, his eyes incandescent, and he smelled like sardines. Sitting at the edge of a barnacle-studded rockpool, the merman Indigo greeted the Countess in his usual way: *"Countessa!"* His voice was melodic, and sometimes when he spoke he would fiddle with the scar on his shoulder where he had once been harpooned.

"Did you find her, Countessa?" the merman Indigo asked.

"No," she responded, wondering once again why he left his mer-mates, who were over there in some other glittering rockpool, and waited impatiently for her. "I might have more luck if you told me her name. Or anything else about her," Countess Fabulosa added.

"No need, when I can tell you what she sounded like," he brushed his hand through the water and picked up a crab, its hard shell glinting in the moonlight, and then he sang. But when he opened his mouth it was not the merman Indigo's voice that emerged. It was the voice of a crowd singer, middle-aged, hoarse but beautiful, a human, a woman, not a case of impersonation or replication but *being*. It was her – the singer – as if he had swallowed her and there she was on his tongue singing, singing as she had done all those years ago on the pier.

"I still don't understand why you want to find this lady."

"Just to tell her how wonderful her singing was."

"She's probably dead. It was fifty years ago and humans don't live as long as mer-people, you know."

The merman Indigo blinked and then shook his head, touching his silvery hair. He had salt-studded violet lashes. From far away she could hear his mer-mates chatting and laughing.

"Fine, I'll walk along the pier again. Plus I'm sick, you know. I can only do so much, Indigo."

"My name's Inigo!" he laughed, and ducked away.

The Countess Fabulosa walked to the pier. She might have had a liking for this kind of adventure in the past when she was well but it provided little happiness now, and she did not (despite Indigo's explanations) understand the need for him to find a pier-singer from half a century ago, nice voice or not. Mer-people, she reckoned, had to have easier lives than humans, if this was all that bothered them. But Indigo – there was something hopelessly magical about him. It made this dreary seaside place tolerable and she thanked her lucky stars she had been staring out of the window at the right time, three days ago, to hear his rockpool song from one hundred floors up.

By now the pier was deserted, and even the karaoke man was gone. What the merman Indigo said wasn't hopelessly far-fetched. It was a small town, and there was a small chance the singer was still alive somewhere. Countess Fabulosa didn't really believe it, but she trudged along the pier with her hands in her dressing gown pockets. The merry-go-round was dark, its noble and skewered horses were silent, and the pier smelled like chips. The wooden slats under her feet seemed too far apart, and the sea under there was vicious and screamingly cold. There was nobody around. The lampposts creaked in the wind. This was the second time Countess Fabulosa had trudged along the pier in two days, carrying out this strange favour for the merman Indigo. She was a little bored.

Eventually Countess Fabulosa reached the part of the pier where the karaoke man had stood, just outside the octagon arcade. This time Countess Fabulosa glanced into the shadowed windows of the bar, and saw a row of photographs tacked to the windows. Countess Fabulosa stared. The photographs were cobwebbed and grimy. There were inscriptions but it was too dark to read them. She shrugged, and was about to turn and head home when she heard, from behind, a set of thundering footsteps. Murderous footsteps. Carnivorous footsteps. There was nowhere to run in her pathetic sanatorium slippers. Even if she had good shoes she could not run for the bus let alone for her life. A goner, a goner! To jump? To swim?

"Countess *Fabulosa*. We've been looking everywhere for you." Nurse Nelson and three sanatorium workers clomped down the pier. They were accompanied by a dog with glow-in-the-dark-eyes and without waiting for an explanation, bundled her into a golf buggy with a flat tyre which trundled tragically back to the sanatorium.

The following morning, three things broke – the waves, Countess Fabulosa's fever, and Countess Fabulosa's heart. Merman Indigo was gone. She had looked out of the window, as she always did, and saw that his rockpool was still and believed he would not return. Nurse Nelson swept into the room with an unacceptable amount of energy for seven o'clock in the morning.

"Count Fabulo called; he's ordered you a clown."

"A clown?"

"Wish I knew more, but I don't. There's a clown coming up in half an hour. He's meant to be good, though," Nurse Nelson continued, leaning over Countess Fabulosa and reaching for a stack of empty medicine packets. That was when Countess Fabulousa's hand shot up and grabbed the golden glinting chain.

"What are you doing?" Nurse Nelson said, holding her necklace so that Fabulosa would not break it. She found it inconceivable that Countess Fabulosa, one of the richest people in the world, with all treasures imaginable available to her (yes, she had seen brochures of the *Merry Celeste,* with its twelve ballrooms and on-board aquarium) should care for this cheap necklace.

"Who's that?" Countess Fabulosa said, pointing at the picture in the pendant.

"My lovely mother. Sang songs on the pier just there, and did it wonderfully too! Long ago, though."

Countess Fabulosa let go of the necklace and Nurse Nelson stood up and smoothed her clothes. "Would you like to – would you like to –" Countess Fabulosa began, but her sentence went nowhere. She didn't know what to ask or how to ask it. The merman Indigo was probably gone, and even if he wasn't, how could she explain it? Countess Fabulosa didn't know what was the right thing to say. She didn't know what was the wrong thing to say. Nurse Nelson waited patiently but Countess Fabulosa turned her face and said nothing. The nurse shook her head sympathetically and bustled around the room, thinking the poor lady to be very ill indeed. Good thing there was a clown coming shortly, she thought, sweeping up some stray seaweed as she left the room.

Martha Glaser

We sat at anchor, hardly moving. The others had gone for a swim to the shore to cool off. Shawn and I stayed on the boat.

"I know what lives in that sea," Shawn said as he began to wind in his line. "You wouldn't catch me in there." His lure glinted silver, just below the surface, as he wound it in. He pulled in out of the water, then with a flick of the wrist, dropped it 50m off the stern, without looking.

Shawn made his living from the sea. He had been out on his boat that morning and was heading out again before dawn. He had joined us for something to do with the day. Fishing was his life.

"The only thing I seem to catch at the moment is sunburn. But that's why they call it fishin' and not catchin'." He put it down to several factors. "Climate change. A lot of the stock moved north. Overfishing. Trawlers taking everything, wrecking the reefs. Then there's just plain bad luck."

As he brought his lure back to the boat again, I was struck by how it moved in the water like an actual fish. "Maybe you need a different lure," I said as something to say.

"This is me best. It was given to me by a mermaid."

I looked toward the beach and said nothing.

"They do exist," he said, answering the question I never bothered to ask.

"Really," I said, dipping my hat into the sea, placing it on my head, and breathing in sharply with the shock of the cold, refreshing, water.

The others had reached the shore, giggling and splashing. I regretted my decision not to go with them, as I sensed a fisherman's tale brewing.

"I met one once," he said. I said nothing. "It were a day a bit like this. The sea were as calm as you get it. Hot and muggy. The fish weren't bitin'. There was a thunderstorm brewin'. I were fishing for bass. Had four rods out. Not so much as a bite.

"Saw her. Bobbin' in the water. Smilin' at me."

"A mermaid? With a tail?"

"Don't be stupid. You'll be going on about unicorns next. They have legs just like you an' me. She were a long way out. I brought the boat alongside and invited her aboard, gave her a towel, some overalls and a mug of lukewarm coffee. I knew she were special straight away. I mean, she were a looker for a start. Then her hair stood on end."

I raised an eyebrow.

"There were an electric storm brewing. It were all the static in the air. Then it started to move in the breeze as the atmosphere changed. The sun caught her face and there was dark clouds coming in behind her. She laughed. I were hooked.

"Then I felt something, like someone had passed a blow torch in front of me forehead. 'Did you see that?' she said, 'a flash of lightning just shot in front of you and went out to sea.' She laughed. "Then one of the rods started to bend. Then another. Then they all went."

"So there we was, the two of us, pulling bass in like they just couldn't help from throwing themselves on the hooks. In the end we had ten rods out. And all around, the lightning were striking the waves. Hitting everything but us. Then the rain came down in buckets. And she just kept on laughing. We got drenched. She stole my heart.

"After that, she moved in. Just kept on laughing. Like she didn't take anythin' serious. And all the time, my luck stayed the same. I couldn't help but catch whatever I went fishing for."

He pulled the lure out of the sea again with perfect timing and held it in his hand for a moment. "Then one day, she left. No reason. Just wasn't there one morning." It seemed to twitch and dance and wriggle on its own. Like it was alive and eager to get back in the water. "Left a note and an envelope. The note said, 'This will be your luck as long as your love lasts.' In the envelope were this lure." He flicked it 60m off the starboard side.

"I looked out for her, whenever the sea were calm. But I never saw her again.

"'Ventually, I stopped looking."

He started to wind in the lure once more, just as the others arrived back at the boat and started to climb aboard.

"Now, it seems, I can't even get a bite on the damn thing."

Just as he spoke, there was a sudden weight on the line and the rod bent.

"You've got one!"

"Rocks," he said.

"Looks like a thunderstorm is brewing," John said, taking the helm. "Let's get the anchor up and get back before we get drenched."

The others dried themselves off and got the boat ready. Shawn stood there, staring at his line at the point where it entered the sea. The engine started and we began to move. There was a sharp clicking sound as Shawn's reel started to give outline. He watched it feed out. Then, slowly, he brought his weather-worn hand round to the top of the reel and pushed it down, firmly. The line stopped. Then snapped, leaving the lure where it belonged, and we headed back to port.

Guy Jones

A SNAIL'S PACE BEAM OF LIGHT
'What would it be like for a person to travel on a beam of light?'
Albert Einstein

Hold on, weird wanderer,
Einstein posed it as a question
not a travel option.
So entertain this on your light excursions:
a snail's pace beam of light
and local Proxima no nearer;
to leave but never arrive,
so no return,
and without death's compensations;
to be the instant's here-and-not-here,
presence and non-presence
in an instant ages long
in the instants unending,
and come your millionth year, mere days advanced;
and in that sink of stasis
no object of admiration for the mind.
This would not be experience.

Perhaps the grave's excursion
holds some delight compared to this
and, sluggish though, would mark more progress too.
We'll pass through things mutable,
in a homelier dark space
to quicken in an earthly light.
I'll never see Andromeda.

Philip Dunn

An endless train heads for the coast, alive with restless children. They have hands that know sand as well as the scrape of their own tongues and feet that itch to be flippers. To be human, after all, is simply to be caught between gill-less fish and flightless bird, in search of metamorphosis for the price of a cheap day return. I listen to the voices in the rattling rails as metal mutters in its allotted role, and I count the rolling wheels until I fall into a deep sleep. The world is a white room stretching forever, in which a sad chansonnier overemotes as he mimes to a wind-up gramophone. Jazz hands sign loss but my French isn't up to understanding the words. There are tears – *lots* of tears – which flood to the horizon, and the singer takes off his shoes and socks and rolls his trousers to his scrawny knees. A foghorn hoots and I wake with a start at a level crossing where an endless train saws the road in half, with old, old men and women mouthing at the windows like earthbound gulls or beached fish. Their veins are filled with saltwater and their skin scratches beneath feathers. It's miles to the coast and the train goes on forever.

Oz Hardwick

Train Journey in Rajasthan

Clamorous heat at Jaipur station –
echoing harsh.
I hustle aboard, find
peace in my carriage.
An old man welcomes me, in his sunset-pink turban,
benign eyes framed by orchid-pink glasses.
We chat in English, as the train rattles on
piercing dry infinity –
suddenly refreshed
by buffalo-flecked waters;
watch a girl-mother
gaze at her sleeping son in silence.
He wakes, leaping on wooden seats.
Gorgeous, in silver *kurta-pajamas*.

                    * * *

Kindness of Strangers

Green crystallised sweets from Varanasi
sucked on a ten hour train journey
all the way to Delhi.

Intimacy of hot wood, and dust.

That cup of *chai*
a Sikh man silently gave to me.

Susan Sciama

THE THOMAS HARDY SAT. NAV.
('We wanted to see Hardy's cottage but the Sat Nav couldn't find it':
overheard snippet of conversation)

Take the London Road out of the Vale.
Ignore the by-ways, the orchards, the meadows – all dead-ends –
and the dreaming spires on your distant left
are not for the likes of you, young Jude.
Get professional training. The future calls.

When convenient make a U-turn.
Your head was filled with grand designs, city ambition,
but they cut no ice with a countryman.

Continue along the Casterbridge Road.
Back to your roots, your dark obsessions.

Take the first exit for Lyonesse.
Go west where the rugged land gives out
to jagged cliffs and salted spray.
Beauty opens its door to you. A pair of blue eyes.
Here is the key to the marriage prison –
in sickness and in stealth, in novels and in verse.

Your pen has re-made the scenery,
transformed the solemn villages,
doomed the yokels to costume drama.

Your route can no longer be computed.
We cannot find your homely church,
the Mellstock band, the kneeling oxen,
your precious heath or that furrowed brow
of the puzzling God you always hated
for not existing.

You will need to download the Wessex App.

You are now officially a tourist attraction
and, although you never expected this ...

... You have reached your destination.

Martin Reed

TRACEY EMIN'S SHOE, FOLKESTONE
(Black and white photograph by Sarah Lodge)

I find you in Ramsgate.
I want you to be true.

A solitary
nameless plimsoll,

the tread flush with
damp compacted gravel,

the upper weathered,
flaking paint.

Your frame holds
chains of association,

room enough
for a dozen backstories.

Hilaire

KURT COBAIN IN WHITELY BAY

After he faked his own suicide
Kurt Cobain left the bright lights of Seattle behind.
He abandoned the good old US of A
to set up a pub in Whitley Bay.

Called the Smells-Like-Teen-Spirits bar,
there he pulled foamy McEwans by the pint.
Sometimes late on he just sat by the door
or outside where he smoked a joint.

And when customers said, are you really him?
Are you that famous guy, that rock star?
He shook his head, replied with a grin,
said No, I'm just someone who runs a bar.

Then he stared at the fret on the icy North Sea
or across the car park at his old Ford Capri,
humming some tune he'd written that day,
Kurt Cobain in his pub in Whitley Bay.

Ian Chapman

Spring sunshine sang through Waverley's
cathedral glass roof and the train was full.
Edinburgh to Newcastle: the one
that does *not* ban booze.

A carriage of lads, aisle-packed
in their pub-on-wheels,
hefty bodies taking up too much space,
lifting cans, putting each other down
with cheery aggression, that camaraderie
of insults and laughter as the train moves off.

One carriage along, three tables of lassies;
hot pink tees with Ellie's Hen Night
in silver lettering, plastic champagne glasses.
They hand out red-iced cupcakes topped
with chocolate penises to other passengers,
their shrill laughter is window cracking.

The East Lothian landscape opens
around us. Bundled into our own small nation,
we follow the blue-grey sea edge,
normal life in suspension;

for an hour and a half these horizons
are one big 'what if'. As they sup and laugh
they know it will soon all be closed off,
but for one night, there's freedom.

Ruth Aylett

is worth running along just for its name.
Unsplendoured stonework, tall terrace,
every house a mottled history. A girl in black peers
down at me from an attic window, and I almost wave –

it might be my grandmother, Elsie. Sent North, put out
in service, she scratches letters home, and embroiders
herself with silk knots into the reverse side of Edinburgh.
Cap properly angled, mop-swiping and stain-blotting,
on her knees she scours prayers into the hierarchy of stairs.

Here she comes – afternoon off – up the basement steps,
a single bar on each shoe fastened with a button,
that damson velvet cloche verging on pert.
I hurry over to follow her, but few can keep pace
with a young woman unfurling after a thirsty spell –

running is more than endurance, than yearning,
breath by breath, it's a form of eloping;
all we have and live is this body,
its voice stirring, breaking loose on the heady road.
Oh, let us release shoulders and straighten spines,
run lofty on the downhill, lengthen our stride, Elsie and I –
let us run together once, a minor disturbance on Great Stuart Street.

Anne Ryland

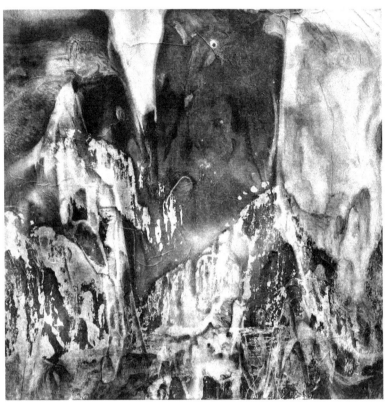

Ice Cliff Ledge

A Tea Shop in Bandon

Someone has left a wet tea-spoon in the sugar
A bluebottle has drowned in the milk
The typical check tablecloth is a mess with breakfast stains
And there's apricot jam smeared on my seat.

But the sunlight that blazes the window
Brings a healthy pink hue to my face
And all the lively domestic noises
Make this tea shop a charming little place.

Owen O'Sullivan

IN AMSTERDAM

My God you must have been so cool
Shooting up in a squat
In Amsterdam, in 1962.

Fresh out of art college you flew
One duffel bag is all you brought
With you, you must have felt so cool.

A sheet, some ink, a bunch of brushes strewn
Amid the ash, the crumbs, the bags of pot
(So cheap to purchase, on the street, in '62).

You smeared the peeling walls: a howl of hues
Of grey and black, back then your manic scrawl
Made everybody think you cool –

The girls queued up to sleep with you
But you had better things to do
Too cool to waste your time on sex in '62

So cool you thought that you could fly; you flew
Four floors, till you were caught
On someone's balcony. My God you were a lucky fool
In Amsterdam, in 1962.

Katie Campbell

The Visitor to the Mountain Refuge

The team *Die Jugend*, six young men, in 1894,
attempt the very first ascent of the dreaded Jägerhorn.
This night, they're on a schnapps-filled bender to dull their painful sores.

Beside the Bergschrund's might they shelter in a hut.
At near to zero Fahrenheit no living things are out.
The night scrapes up the very twilight and slams the long day shut.

From their phonograph there drones Act One of Das Rheingold.
But then they hear an awful moaning. That's "W-a-ä-agner!" guffaws
Berthold.
"Tshhh", said Karl, counting pitons, "This bit's just instrumental".

A pounding on the door halts conjecture then louder and louder the
blows.
The oak implodes and the temperature plummets. Then from the shadows
emerges a cadaverous creature still shedding gobs of snow.

Its face is pale; a shocking eyeful. And its fingers bleed.
There is an overpowering smell of wet and mouldy tweed.
"Mein Gott, es ist der Teufel". Herr Feigling spills his tea.

Its ropes hang and its pans clang; its lips are thin and blueish.
Gustav screams and recoils in angst as if it were something ghoulish.
The visitor's gibbering in some language, Ernst says, might be
"Englisch".

It shambles in, collapsing on the tomato soup tureen.
Spattering all in red contagion across the room it careens.
It gobbles up their spaghetti rations like some horror scene.

Attempts to stop it come to nought. Karl suggests an axe.
More wisely, Dr. Martini remarks, let's try a shot of schnapps;
or let's sing the carol *Stille Nacht* until it does collapse.

In the dead of night an alarm clock rings. It's many hours before dawn.
With expedition members groaning and their faces pale and drawn
they watch the walker rise, crushing Gustav's compass with its crampons.

Gustav complains: *"Unless I'm misled, he shows no sign of remorse".*
"Which way?" asks Karl of the aforesaid as he lumbers out the door.
"He goes my friend, but steadily, toward the Jägerhorn".

Clifford Liles

Party on Scutchamer Knob

Ceaselessly we skin the night
down to the wishbones of our dreams.

Clouds slip, smoke drifts and clings
to sweaty hand-knits; the reek of freedom.

Green wood pops and oozes
flames silent, articulate,

old stories eagerly using up
the hoard of wood,

crack and whistle punctuation,
tales wind-blown, glowing.

We grunt pagan platitudes
Dope will get you through ... Never trust a man in a ...

Our senses spin until they curdle
with the curly smoke,

sparks of meaning lance upward
winking out above our heads.

Sifting the soft ash of morning for our memories;
we should listen to the fire.

Ivan McGuinness

WHEN

and when one of us is dying we may remember the day we walked
the long miles by the estuary. the strength of the wind meant we
couldn't face the water but had to sit on the sheltered side of the
embankment. we counted six different types of butterfly. a peacock.
a couple of whites. two small orange ones we couldn't identify and
a dark one almost black. the sun came out for a minute or two and
and we ate fruit and flapjacks and laid back and kissed. later we
got up and holding hands walked on again not towards the ends of
our lives but towards the end of the walk. and we talked and i wasn't
thinking of the future as you pointed to a field of barley to some scots
pines to a jetty where a tanker called 'buccoo reef' was moored. and
when one of us is dying we may recall all this and how later the
tanker slipped away in the dark.

Andy Fletcher

Autumn Pudding

Why do I seek this satisfaction
of wooden spoon and china bowl,
blending oranges, eggs and spices,
stirring up spells, brief enchantments,
as I follow your longhand recipe?

We'd eat this after roast Welsh lamb,
November Sunday afternoons.
Yummy! you write at the end of the page
and I want to hear your voice at my shoulder,
the punch and heft of that northern vowel.

I read your diaries, times gone forever,
plant a tree to grow from your ashes,
hear all the words we should have said,
false re-creations, blundering acts
ways of placating, pretending, prolonging

but food seems practical not mawkish,
a celebration with fresh ingredients.
This meal won't be a sacrament,
only a whiff of *temps perdu*
to heal a past, hold back a future,

take me back to Worcestershire walks
through windfalls in forgotten orchards,
kicking up leaves when no-one was looking,
a honeyed harvest maturing and mellow,
bittersweet tang of love on the tongue.

Martin Reed

DELICATESSEN

A place full of promises. Food
as benediction, sacraments
from foreign ceremonies of sun.

Frittata, chorizo, dolmades
were your vocabulary of grace,
pungencies of herbs and garlic

your incense. Your stained glass
cheeses from white Époisses to orange
Mimolette, and multiple reds of salami.

Culture, history and sophistication
to take home, for stories starting
'I first tasted this in a little village ...'

But it's all too late now.
No more of that foreign rubbish,
we must worship the Full English.

Ruth Aylett

BASKET CASE

Rhubarb, bi-carb
Kit-kats, lemon tea
Chocolate ice-cream, Boots sunscreen
Bottled beer
And TCP.

Cornflakes, vac-shakes
Dog food, frozen peas
Chicken chowders, Beecham's powders
Superglue
And processed cheese.

Fruitcake, fresh hake
Pritt stick, olive oil
Piccalilli, tubs of Philly
Pineapples
And Bacofoil.

Mince wipes? Wax bites?
Fish spray? Cat glue?
Crisp spaghetti? Hot confetti?
Dettol chunks?
I'm confused.

Minerone? Macastroni?
Carpet paste? Gravy World?
Trolley's heaving, must be leaving
Take me to the check-out girl.

Ken Gambles

MILLET

From field to field, your eyes needled their hayrick stalks;
your fingers crackled and darkened to charcoal sticks.

Stitching slogged bodies into the roots of their sowing tracks,
you watched wintry blood blacken to a stubble-burnt bruise.

Fog chewed slowly on a rind of old sun. Long nights stacked
to blank the horizon. Edgings of light flashed their blades,

blindly, blunted, to whet each new moon's crescence.
Somewhere a sickle would swing so the darkness bled.

John Andrew

BEETROOT

A kidney harvested from a refugee
by a Russian widow in Knightsbridge.
When cut, that trickled blood
is its last sigh. How can a superfood
taste like dirt and turn your urine red?
Don't put any in my sandwich.
Cold, it's a corpse on the slab,
waiting for the post-mortem.

Stuart Pickford

HARVEST

These beans we sow between ourselves
will not feed me.
Before they tent the canes, trap summer's
shadow in a circle of damp black soil,
before Helen plucks the long green fingers with her own,
catches them in the scoop of her apron (will a wooden peg still
be in the pouched pocket?)
I, according to all things,
the best guess of all these things
by people who know of all these things,
will have been plucked myself.

Ivan McGuinness

To name you simply *brown* is a disservice.
An *essence*, shall we say,
more substrate than the finished article,
a secret ingredient
that gives the dish its authenticity and vim.

Viewed from a top deck,
the squares and polygons of fields
are chequered with promise,
your wherewithal for beans and barley spikes,
that Summer meadow.

Too subtle to figure in a rainbow,
you fleck the everywhere.
Richard of York chose primaries in vain.
Imagine a world of underlying indigo!
You are the colour seen by so-called colour-blind.

You make your stand pigmentially
in most of what surrounds us –
turf and tilth and seashore,
base tone for the gold brocades of Autumn,
sparrows', eagles', thrushes' wings.

Best forgotten, the hideous decade
that flattened colour in uninspired geometries –
brown this, matte that – they call it *vintage* now.
You mock it with your tubes of colour
squeezed at squat, then flushed away.

Gerald Killingworth

BAMBOOZLED IN MAY

Oh, here the sun and golden buttercups,
Nay, now the rain and pesky gales

Well, I tell you there are few things more troublesome,
Than the presence of an uncertain day.

Ah, the songsters high in the chestnut tree,
Sharing for all their heavenly art

Low my cry and crushed spirit that sits in me,
When cruel winds cause them to depart.

Owen O'Sullivan

RED GROUSE

From the tangle of the undergrowth –
that throaty chatter, slowing
to a half laugh; then how
they seem to speak –
go back, go back, go back.

But today it is the Glorious Twelfth.
Coming into earshot, the beaters' feet
interrogate the heather,
scare the nestling grouse
into a fleeing airborne exodus.

Each shooter trains his sights
onto a skylit silhouette.
Yards up: lead pellets
sing like midges, below:
a plummeting of dead birds.

These are the moments
those panting gun dogs
have been bred for. They bring
the limp birds in like slippers
to their masters' feet.

The hunters' jagged words
compete and mingle
with the wind.
Toe caps kick past
spent red cartridges.

Now their banter slowly dies away
back along their tracks
through the trodden grass to where
their car doors slam
against the voiceless heath.

Greg Smith

RED BIRD SPOTTED BY Z-GEN YOUTH

inside this shoot of wood inside this city
I rattled off the script of this preserve

here beyond these trees above their scalps
see the forest tower peering back

but gazing West, you spied the bird instead
a cardinal lit up among gray winter branch

how had I missed such bright slash of spirit
when looking for that one stick of structure

I stare forever inward the texture of order
while you see everything else that moves

Corbett Buchly

TO A FLY

We share the same square feet of air:
this kitchen equal with a festering bog,
a road kill, a humming cow field.

While I try to look toward the stars,
Your guiding light is putrefaction,
things lying at the very bottom of the heap.

You breed by outnumbering the prodigious rate
of your mortality; too many white and writhing maggots
striving to be alive.

You are sufficient for your own purposes;
you live on what must finally remain of us.
You will inherit the earth.

You are the exact embodiment
of every other fly: your ravenous proboscis, black-bristled legs,
pleasing only to another fly.

You live without belief.
You have no poetry or music, no prayers. There is no weeping
over the spent shell of your carcass.

You live inside each teeming microsecond.
among bacteria and motes of dust. Yesterday, tomorrow
are distant galaxies.

Even now, in some close zone, your blue metallic fuselage
is scrawling an unsettling moan and stutter
on the air.

Nothing can keep up with your mid-air rat runs.
I furl the world news into a paper cudgel.
You have moved before I even think.

Greg Smith

My pockets are heavy with the weight of shadows. I think it's a matter of age. Where once they'd come and go – from sunlight, to tungsten, to neon, to moonlight – now they just hang around, like old policemen at crime scenes who've forgotten that they were the victims. For a while, there were so many that I could barely see, and I'd take a circle of darkness with me wherever I went, which was fine in the cinema but less so at weddings, or when collecting my children from the school gate. But then I learned how to peel them off flat surfaces and tuck their edges in on themselves, over and over, until they could no longer be seen by the human eye, or even with the microscope I was given for my seventh birthday. The density is one of those numbers that's just marks on paper, that the human brain can't comprehend, and there's more, and more, and more and more andmore andmoreandmoreandmore each time I experience the proximity of light. There's a black hole in my pocket, dear Liza, dear Liza, and it's drawing me back to the scene of unspeakable crimes.

Oz Hardwick

you take a walk in Brockwell Park
to get away from the cobwebs

the warm wind tangles with your hair
too thin now

you scale the hillock to reach the view
breathless

stand among the trees
look north over the petrol haze

to the sparkling towers
craving their uplift

but today they lean
unsteady

must be the curvature of the Earth

the parakeets squawk and squabble above you
you wonder how they got here

this gaudy green flock
all the way from the tropics

below a child with a kite that will not fly
you had one like that

you ran and ran
but it never took off

back home you sit for a while
in the threadbare armchair

gather the energy to make a cup of tea

you notice the small case
packed and ready in the corner
forgetting for a moment why it's there
you fill the kettle

see a kite flying above the park
hope it's that child's

wish her well

Bel Wallace

Builders, you say. Predictably:
You scoff at Lapsang and Earl Grey.
Sugar? One. No half! That's a very large spoon!
(I'm trying to signal sweetness, or perhaps generosity)

Milk? You nod
And together we watch as the thin stream of white slowly penetrates the
brown
Disappearing altogether
Till suddenly it rises, marbling the surface.

Nuage, I think. I want to tell you this:
The French would say a nuage, a cloud of milk.
Or they'd call it a larme – a tear drop.
But we have no name for this mingling of things

I'm waiting for you to stay stop
But you don't.
So I don't.

I am pouring more and more
Liquid slips over the lip of the cup
Slides onto the counter
Drips on the floor …

Katie Campbell

WHERE I MUST HAVE PUT THE THING

Oh, right, that's where I must have put it. Or
could it have dropped down from an upper drawer?
The bureau feels too full, as life becomes
but mere amounts, strange desultory sums

of circumstance, capricious as a sigh.
Had objects souls, how many hearts might rot
from simple sloppiness! But we can die
of heartbreak; the inanimate cannot.

Aren't memories also things, though? And love grows
through blunt and blurred remembrances I own
because they can't be hurt now, I suppose.
Like stuff in drawers, thrice touched, twice used, once known.

James B. Nicola

THE I WAY

independence begins with an I
not caring how others did
there's no such thing as society, fuck it
I'm on the way, my
way to hell, my way

Terry Sherwood

Silent Cliff Pass

EXCUSE ME

I know the middle seat's the worst
But would you please move your knee?
You're man-spreading in my space,
Can't you see how I'm pressed against
The window, trying to slide out of the way?
We're all asleep, yes, please take your head
From my shoulder; I don't want to know
If you've slipped or snuggled up with intent.
You're heavy; your breath on my neck
Makes me feel sick. Were Mother here
She'd poke you very hard with knitting needles
(Now forbidden in hand luggage, by the way).
I never learned to knit, so just move away, okay!
I know the seats are small; but you, sir,
Are large – please note that I haven't used
Offensive words like *overweight*, *obese* or *fat* –
See how I'm forced to squeeze my elbows tight
While the armrest between us strains
To contain you. I wonder why you do not
Overhang the gentleman on the other side,
Neatly folded in his space; why you'd leave
The overhead light on if you are asleep?
I ring the bell. The cabin crew
Offer an upgrade – not to me, to you.

Anne Eyries

began in corridors and along the skirting boards,
as though it might have slipped under like a bobby pin.

I ripped open the carpet like a stomach, expecting to see
partially digested soil in the shape of a girl.

I squinted at family photos, hoping one was a portal
and I could fall into that smiling body.

I ripped off dolls' heads and stared into their organless torsos,
imagining it in there, a Matryoshka doll.

I climbed inside the mirror and saw shrieking faces
multiplying like fragments in kaleidoscope vision.

I went downstairs, as though I might find it
eating cereal at the kitchen table.

I went in the wardrobe and the clothes whispered.
I smelt decay. It was gone.

So I grew another body, like a sapling
emerging from the darkness.

I dropped every cell of skin that he ever touched.
Hello, body. It's nice to meet you.

Heather Hughes

He hit her in the street where people could see
and they rushed with outrage.

So he fashioned a frame with his finger,
creating a case around him and her.

He drew windows and heavy curtains
which hung like nimbostratus clouds.

He added a roof and a garden with a fence
and colourful flowers climbing

up the railings. He made a door
and shut it. After a while the house

groaned like a tree, every day drooping
lower like an osier until it was inches

from her face so she learnt not to move.
She shared air with the house so rationed

her breath. When she called the police
they said they didn't deal with domestics.

A moving van is a pair of angel's wings.

Heather Hughes

If I could grasp your anger
I would hold onto it firmly.
I'd tame it like a falcon.
put a hood over its head
to calm it and soothe its violence.

If I could teach your anger
I would teach it metallurgy.
It would learn the meaning
of heat and respect its bite.
It would learn to make
the sharpest of blades,
not to injure but instead
to chop vegetables, it would see
that the sharpest blade is required
not for something hard
but for something soft and tender
like slicing tomatoes.

And I'd teach it what is really brave
is to turn itself into forgiveness;
because blades and bombs ricochet back
at their users and inflict many wounds
that are not immediately seen
but leave scar tissue in the soul.

Colin Pink

THE GARDEN AT CASTLECOUNTESS

It steeped steps to a high garden
he grew vegetables either side of,
alternated varieties year by year;
apple trees and strawberries crawled under mesh wiring
that the scalliwags cut through to steal fruit.

The scalliwags grew into brats
that grew into gurriers
that made Grandad's life a misery;

grew into coke-head murderers
doing time for beating the shite out
of my Grandad's life
just because he had no money kept in the house.

Noel King

MOONSET

To the far west you look
as the vanilla moon
turns lemon by the book
then orange. It will soon

be gone like your loved one
and in some span of hours
will tap upon their stone
as if its will were yours.

The few souls you still know
observe your futile task.
*You've sat at this window
how long?* some deign to ask.

But all the nights you've seen
the moon tumesce and set
have not even been
half a century yet.

James B. Nicola

are you bothered by our unneighbourly noise
what do you make of the self-harm
we restless souls do for progress for growth
do you fear colonisation exploitation

our cast shadows make you look as though
you're covering your eyes slowly uncovering them
can't you bear to see us gouge our flesh
poison soil sea air overheat our atmosphere
destroy habitat species

can you do more than bathe our feet with your tides

Terry Sherwood

SEA SKY LAND

a sea that cannot be fished
a border that cannot be crossed

a sky that is owned by drones
a land that is sown with shrapnel

a home and a people blown apart
a world that is deaf, dumb and blind

Colin Pink

A Climate of Hostility
"Because we never stop destroying."
(Ned Beauman: Venomous Lumpsucker)

Two parallel proposals endorsed
By too many of us on planet Titanic:
Deckchairs should be slashed to stop
Self-indulgence at the top or smashed
To stop pig-headedness on lower decks.

But all too soon the iceberg comes,
Obliterates such meaningless distinctions,
Conflict a futile luxury:
No one escapes from the wreckage
When the Antarctic goes into meltdown.

Wilf Deckner

FERN
(After Sylvia Plath, 'Mushrooms')

Weighted footsteps –
Beaten, and battered. Retreat
safely underground.

Nurtured in darkness
under warm moulded blankets.
Slowly we expand.

Delicate, not frail.
Adversity forges our
survival techniques.

Morning dew settles.
Freshly formed fingers begin
to hunt warm sunlight.

Breeze slaloms round Birch.
Stems sway, freshly formed fronds reach
right through the hard ground.

Trampled by man's foot.
Curled up tight, start unfurling
and embrace our light.

Debi Knight

WINTERING

Osiria is a beautiful rose
and yet half shabby
with a ragged look.

She knows the moment hope is gone
the way the world retreats
to a forgotten dream.

She catches every silent scream
and then unfolds
astounding reason.

Her red and ivory lies like wax
stamped in an otherworldly mould
some holy relic flesh and blood.

Her petals melt and when she dies
and crumbles into autumn's damp
the time ahead too long and dark and cold

her name survives
through every season
as if there's something that it holds.

Andria Cooke

of leaves make oxygen,
exhale the substance giving
breath
from which all life is made.
They rise and sway in spring
where empty branches waved
and opening like eyes they breathe and sing.
The Great War's slough of darkness
cracked and crashed the woods
and copses, blasted all the trees till none stood
but ragged wreckage; corpses hanging,
skeletons protruding jagged from the slurry and the mud.
But reason followed shame.
The world turned
and even here in season green regeneration came.
The breathing of the leaves was saved.
Surely we can learn.
While
trees
remain
the world
can change again.

Andria Cooke

AN HOUR WITH MISHA
(i.m. Misha Norland 1943 – 2021)

Pushing open the green door,
bell jangling our arrival,
we step over the threshold
into the calm of the garden,
while the house dreams on
in a haze of lavender wisteria.

Discarding shoes in the porch
we linger in the hall till Misha
beams his smile from the stairs.
I go up first, sink in the sofa –
talk and pause and talk
while Misha probes my thoughts.

I am emptied out,
finally sit back into silence;
Misha considers his options,
taps computer keys, asks
another question, taps again,
selects the matching remedy.

Another hour to linger in the garden,
enclosed by trees and wall,
I wander the paths, absorb birdsong,
watch ducks parade the lawn,
catch the scent of flowers,
drowse with the dreaming house.

Pulling open the green door,
bell jangling our departure,
we step over the threshold,
refreshed, restored, renewed,
Yondercott House and Misha
working their magic together.

Heather Deckner

PROFESSORS

(i)
They got him to explain his thesis to us,
as much guineapigs as students,
the objective of our agreeing met
after a roasting in the academic press
for being the first to dare suggest
Dylan was a poet.

(ii)
Discovering by chance he died
nine years ago, fireworks of memories:
awkwardness at his faculty parties,
blamelessly dumped on another tutor,
saying things that displeased him at dinners.
Now I dig out to read
the book about his son's addictions,
making a belated connection.

(iii)
He was drummed out for heresy,
not seeing eye-to-eye with the theological
college deans. They disliked that he divorced,
even if he did remarry,
and had a different interpretation
of sin that fell foul of their tradition.
But an employment tribunal
vindicated, where facts not faith were discussed.

Niall McGrath

YOUNG ASCHERSON

I saw him on the TV late last night
And recognised him almost instantly –
Young Ascherson. He hadn't changed a bit
Since we were boys at school, oh let me see,
It must be all of forty years ago.
To me he seemed the same, or nearly so.

Mind you, he'd been an odd sort of a boy,
At fifteen, bookish, studious and dull,
Or so I thought. He seemed not to enjoy
The things we did. Serious, respectful.
I can't remember having seen him laugh.
Still, he was popular among the staff.

But age now seemed to suit him perfectly.
Becoming now, that air of gravitas.
The greying hair of seniority
Had transformed that sententious silly ass,
Now comfortably ensconced in middle age,
Into a worldly, well-respected sage.

Somehow with me the trick had been reversed.
In middle-age a fool, I do not shine
At all. It's clear my golden days came first.
Since adolescence I've been in decline
And even Ascherson would laugh to see
What he has made and what time's made of me.

George Jowett

Tivadar Szilard walked through the tenements of Brooklyn, the stench of the streets wafting up his nostrils and permeating his clothes. Filthy urchins ran through the streets, adding a cacophony of noise to the squalor of the neighborhood, making Szilard cringe and draw back into his own skin. He checked the directions on the torn slip of paper he carried in his left hand, then turned south at a street corner where raw sewage oozed from the gutter.

Tivadar Szilard was the World Chess Champion. He was probably the best player who had ever lived.

But he was not The Legend.

The Legend had the improbable name of Guster Boone. He had retired and disappeared twenty years ago after burning through the world of chess like a magnesium flame. Boone had grown up in a middle class neighborhood in a better part of Brooklyn. A child prodigy, he was the youngest Grandmaster in history. After winning the American chess title, he had abruptly ceased tournament play. It was theorized that he had burnt out, that he was a prodigy who would never achieve mature status.

Then came the Magnificent Year. Boone had suddenly risen up, entered the tournament for the World Chess Championship, and had destroyed his opponents in ways that had never been seen in the world of chess. In the semifinals and finals, he demolished his opponents 6-0, 6-0, 9-0, no draws. It had never happened in chess before. It had never happened since.

In the championship match that year, he had destroyed the old Russian who had stood as champion of the world for a decade. The old Russian had continued to perform in tournaments for several years thereafter, but it was universally acknowledged that he was no longer the player he once had been. It was said that the match with Boone had broken something inside him.

The world had hailed Boone, the conquering hero, and proclaimed him invincible.

But he had never played another game. He had never defended his title. He had disappeared from public view. When the next championship tournaments began, he didn't enter. There was much media coverage of the invincible champion who refused to defend his title. There was speculation and editorials, theorizing and psychologizing, predictions of an eventual triumphant return. But as the years passed, the world of chess had sadly moved on.

Then came Tivadar Szilard, the Hungarian phenom. It was said Szilard had the most creative play in the history of the game. He had the highest chess score of anyone who had ever lived. He had read every book ever written on the game and penned a score of them himself. But his entire career had been dogged by the shadow of the former champion. Guster Boone. The Legend.

Szilard stopped in front of the brownstone and checked the address on the slip of paper. He hesitated a moment, then climbed the stoop. He had come to destroy a legend.

A narrow wooden stairway led to the second floor, its steps old and sagging. A bare bulb was the only illumination. Szilard ascended slowly.

The second floor hallway was dark. Though it was midday, the lone window at the end of the corridor allowed little sunlight through its grime. Szilard stopped at a wooden door marked 2A. He knocked.

"It's open," called a voice from within.

Szilard turned the brass knob and pushed the door ajar.

The apartment consisted of a single room. An unmade bed stood in the corner. Dirty dishes cluttered the wooden table and the sink. Piles of magazines lined the walls and scattered across the floor, competing with hills of books. And there, sitting in an ancient cloth chair under a reading lamp, sat the Legend.

Guster Boone was older than any picture Szilard had seen of him. His gaunt face was narrower than it had been in his youth. But it was unmistakably him. Above the light of the reading lamp, Szilard could see the eyes, brilliant and sinister, almost reptilian. The corners of his mouth were turned up in a slight, mocking grin. The two men stared at each other.

"You're Guster Boone," said Szilard; it was not a question.

Boone lowered his head in acknowledgement, the grin deepening, the angle of his eyebrows highlighting the sinister eyes.

"I'm Tivadar Szilard." When Boone gave no answer, Szilard added, "The World Chess Champion."

The reptilian nature of Boone's eyes deepened. The grin became tighter.

"I've come to play you."

Szilard saw no surprise in the man's face, no resentment, no amusement, no emotion of any kind – only a sharp attentiveness.

"I'm not talking about a public tournament," said Szilard. "I mean a private match. Just you and me. No press, no media, no hordes. Just the two best chess players who have ever lived."

Emotion returned to Boone's visage, the sinister amusement. "Tivadar Szilard. I've studied all your games."

"I'll put up any stakes you name," said Szilard. "Offer any prize, any amount. A single game or a match of any length. You set the terms. You set the stakes."

"I don't want your money," said Boone.

"What do you want?"

The sinister glint deepened. "I'll play you. A single game. But on my terms."

Szilard waited. Boone leaned forward.

"The winner will open the head of the loser and eat his brain."

Szilard stared into the madness of Boone's eyes. It was not a joke or a bluff. He meant it. And he saw something else in the mad brilliance of Boone's eyes – a total certainty of what the outcome would be.

Szilard knew that for the rest of his life he would never forget the look in the eyes – or the quality of the laughter that echoed in the narrow shaft of the stairway and only ended when the door closed behind him as he emerged into the street.

Mark Pearce

WIZARD

Kenneth came stooped, unsteady, listened
as I turned the key, inspected
the replacement aux pipe and filters.
He checked the sizes of a few nuts,
rattled wrenches in a toolbox at the back
of the station wagon, slackened
a couple of screws at the side of the block.
When I turned her over again, the airlock
began to clear as spits became streams.
Before long she was roaring like a dream.
Us young lads soon grew bored of hearing
the old boys yacking
like the tractor's start-up clacking,
moseying on up the lane as they stood
until evening air grew chilly against oil-stained
shirts and grey hair and the light diminished
like the cloud of fumes from the vertical
exhaust pipe after pistons were stilled.

Niall McGrath

THE CHURCH OF ST. JOHN THE DENTIST
(On misreading the church's name obscured by leaves, Grainger Street, Newcastle)

Please, just 'John' will do. We'll go
into the Baptistry. I like
to work from there. I'm not sure why.

If you'd care to put these glasses on,
they'll stop unfortunate liquids marring
your view. (Thank you, Salome.)

She's very trustworthy, good at her job,
and of an evening loves to dance.
We'll start by looking for imperfections,

teeth that have gone the wrong way,
that have strayed from good practice.
I have a dedication to my profession,

some will say it borders on
obsessive since I will brook
no deviation from what I consider

to be good behaviour. It may be
that I suffer for this, and if so,
it will be for the greater good. Another

will come who will bring to the wider world
enlightenment, and the greater dentistry.
Sometimes I feel as though I am

a lone voice in the wilderness,
yet I seem to know these things.
All I can do is foretell this coming,

receive into my practice all those
who show themselves receptive to the way.
Well, all seems fine, but please be sure

to maintain vigilance, and look out for
that other I mentioned. Now Salome
will help you with your account, or as she

amusingly calls it, your 'decollation'.
I don't know why. A mystery that girl sometimes.

Malcolm Carson

His cigarette butts still litter the terrace
So casually cast
I wonder if at the time I minded
By then I was blinded, by love? Lust? Desire?
I admired the way he rolled them
– tight little roaches –
While telling us for the third or fourth time
About buying his place in Venice
Or selling his Maserati

Or the way his grandfather escaped the gestapo
Catching the last flight out of Berlin
To Cuba where he kept a flat
In a grand hotel on the Malecon
And sat out the war selling the diamonds
He'd bartered for safe passage:
He must have had an ally inside
Someone who would turn a blind eye
And issue passports, for a fee.

My flat-mate, who was even more hooked than me
Pushed him for ever more details:
Why he had learned to speak Chinese
Or where he got that proverb
About trusting in God but tethering the horses
Getting him to teach her how to roll a fag:
How much hash to sprinkle on the tobacco
Rushing off to the fridge for another cold bottle.
By then I was beginning to wonder:

No comment, no judgement, no shame
He told his tales so matter-of-factly
But it wasn't till he lost his phone
And no longer called me at dawn
Drawling *Good Morning Darling*
That the spell really broke for me.
Darling, I blush to think that's all it took
Despite the disappearances
Days at a time. And the volatility

– A polite word for random acts of violence.
Perhaps that's overstating it:

Let's call it casual abuse …
Or perhaps it was simply negligence
Perhaps it wasn't that at all
Just different expectations …
With distance it gets harder to recall.
I've forgotten most of the stories
But I do remember he replied

When I asked what happened to the cash
That his grandfather did okay:
They say that he kept camels on Long Island.

Katie Campbell

Snow Obscured Heights

'SHE WEARS HER CLOTHES, AS IF THEY WERE THROWN ON WITH A
PITCHFORK'
(Jonathan Swift)

Her dress
is an abandoned house
and she the only squatter.
Her shoes moulder
like drowned puppies.

Her shawl
teems with grubs
and peckish birds.
Her ears sprout
wild poppies.

In her slumbers
she is fleet
and stark,
riding the cosmos
unencumbered.

On waking
she grabs her pitchfork,
chucks on some clothes,
sallies forth
for more adventures.

Hilaire

THE GAZE

I like that look in my eyes
after a few glasses of reasonably expensive white
at that new stylish West Village restaurant
on a lazy Saturday afternoon

from the other side of the mirror
a woman looks straight back at me
her eyes
intensely wild
with a certain kind of sensual expectation
the look of pure bravery
enticing
as if the whole universe was able to fit into one gaze.

Jagoda Olender

FRIENDSHIPS ARE COMPLICATED

in the flames of a bonfire
our friendship died
under the night sky
and the silent judgement of the stars
our glances encompassed
the power of forever
while our lips
were still dripping with regret

I bottled that moment in my memory
as I knew this will be
the last friendly look and touch
we will ever exchange.

Jagoda Olender

END

A day after everything that has passed,
the bees are waiting when I return,
and a footpath leads across the meadow
to the nest they built in a sycamore,
well used by those who come to whisper.

Their song is now wistful, evoking
histories of triumph and tragedy,
related by people who came back
with news of love and separation,
happiness and loss.

We have learned, they hum,
that one follows the other,
that beginnings have ends
but ends precede beginnings.

William Coniston

THE THIRD STEP

The early hours call for him
again; duvet skewed,
pillows flat, curtains
listing to one side.

In the attic room, sleep
surrounds their daughter.

Despite his woollen socks,
cold starts to grip:
varicose veins itch,
capillaries shrink, blood
struggles with the heart.

He pulls his body from the bed
for his dressing gown,
hanging behind the door.

That's when he knows
the girl he met at nineteen
in dungarees and DMs
isn't coming back:
two steps and a stride
took him over the floorboard
that squeaked down and up;
leaving her free to dream:
her calm, easy face.

Tonight, his foot lands
on the creaking groan.
Like standing on a mine,
he freezes in empty space.

Stuart Pickford

When I was young:
Sticks, stones, a feather from a bird.
Objects that spoke to me,
As a child from the heart.

Then as a teen:
Gum, mascaras, lipsticks of vanity,
Exiled these,
An imposition from above.

Standing here now,
In the park,
As a woman,
Once again, my pockets are joy-filled with sticks, stones, a feather
from a bird.
Objects that have returned to me,
From my heart.

Carmella de Keyser

LUNCH HOUR IN THE STATIONERY CUPBOARD

Sometimes I find a quiet place
and have a moment on my own
indulging in the artist's ways,
avoiding the congestion zone,

tune in my mind, turn off my phone,
a pen and paper close at hand,
I write for me and me alone
for no one else would understand

the ramblings of a journeyman
who keeps this secret safe in case
the only way to wonderland
is hiding in a quiet place.

Simon Tindale

OUR CASTLES
(after Gill Knight)

Our laughter pours from monochrome.
Plimsolls grubby, shorts baggy, we are ragged-
edged, but fully auntied by hand-knitted jumpers.
We prod and scoop, tap and flump.
Dig deeper moats, mound taller towers.
Solid bungalow children, uncramped beside water,
hollering and wrangling. Happy to abandon
our crooked castles – their simple collapse.
On our sludge-creek of the Thames, chimneys
belch from the other side. Grey patches
crisping on our cheeks, ultraviolet not known.
Our parents rig defences from worry and love alone.

Those years, guarded by rules and walls,
we returned over and over to shores apart,
to the pinkish hues of warning skies, to spots
of light far out, or not so far. Though we'd grown
softly spoken, we called to each other tide by tide.
In a lower corner where we'd never gone,
we retrieved a ruin; its flag smudged, untorn.
Hungry still for egg and cress rolls,
we could no longer huddle. Haar seeped into us,
our faces sea-washed into similar patterns.
Whenever I left home, I would touch the slumped
castle as if it were our lintel, to keep us all from harm.

Anne Ryland

It causes me no small amusement to think about it now, but there was a time when I actually could not wait to go home for the summer. In particular, it was in my fifteenth year that I had my most acute attack of nostalgic fervour. These were the heady days before mobile phones had made every place and every person instantly accessible, and, as a consequence, indistinguishable. No, in our grotty provincial boarding school we were utterly alone, and left completely to our imaginations. In the folly of my youthful seclusion, I started to re-imagine my home – an unassuming dairy farm in the Carnic Alps – as an Arcadian dreamscape, where the people and the animals were in tacit communion, where nobody spoke but in enigmatic parables, where life was conducted at the drowsy pace of a trickling stream and not the relentless heart-pound of a mechanical clock, and where everyone's skin was radiant with the afterglow of an honest life's work – even the children. How easily was my memory subordinated to fantasy!

On the day of my departure, I was almost overflowing with anticipation. Even then I considered myself quite a measured person, but I recall that on this particular day my uncharacteristic giddiness prompted me to say all kinds of frivolous things that I rather wished I hadn't. I laughed harder than I was wont, surprised everyone with my sudden onset of volubility, and every last person I took my leave of added a fresh tear to my rapidly moistening eye (even the ones I hated, which at that point in the semester was pretty much all of them). I was going home, at last, to my cradle of revitalisation.

When I saw my father's car pull up outside the boarding house, I seized my luggage and sprinted into the foyer. The morning sun streamed so rapturously through the east-facing windows that the place looked like it could have been the waiting room for Heaven. There they were, on the other side of the portal, too timid to come in. I opened the door and motioned them to enter. Mother did so begrudgingly, Father flat out refused. They had that characteristically bewildered look of rustics in a metropolis, and I rejoiced in their simplicity – at how closely they comported to my prefabricated image. They were dressed as they always were: Father in a checked shirt and jeans; Mother in a frock and apron, with a kerchief to boot.

'Hello, sweetheart,' whispered Mother, picking up my suitcase. 'Let's take this outside.'

When we came outside, she hugged and kissed me with her accustomed vigour. Father simply eyed my suitcase suspiciously.

'You'll have to sit with that on your lap; we need to leave enough room for the pigs,' he said.

'I beg your pardon?' said I.

'The pigs.' He looked at me blankly, as if I should have known what he was talking about. 'We have just bought three little pigs.'

With the ire of an enlightened cuckold, I made straight for the car boot, and did indeed find three tender little piglets expectantly glowering at me through the glass. I might have been apoplectic if I had not been so astonished. I put down my suitcase to get a better look, only to find my father's prohibiting hand barring my way to the boot handle.

'Don't open it,' he said, and by his implacable countenance I saw that the man could never in his life be made to comprehend the indignity he had just done me, so foreign was his view of the world to mine. Any stirrings of anger in me melted like wax in light of this innocent ignorance – it would have been like begrudging a baby for belching.

I opened the back door and heaved in my suitcase, and was duly welcomed with a searing blast of oven-hot air to the face. It was a very hot day. Then a second, more insidious, sensory assault; namely the fetid stench of cloistered livestock, which carried with it all my heretofore dormant memories of frustration and monotony and censure and control, less as a procession of recollected events than a stifling ambience; a reminder of the person I was then, and how depressingly little that piteous wretch differed from the person I was now.

The piglets moved about only very occasionally, but made a great clamour in their kinetic quietism, treating us to a medley of squeals, sniffles and grunts; and I like to imagine that there was an absolute division of labour between the three, with one supplying all the squeals, another serving as the solitary sniffler, and the third the sole purveyor of grunts. As we drove out of town and into the sticks, green spaces suddenly started to emerge and then recede from the relentlessly reconfiguring vista of the car window. All manner of things came into view: fields that were forbidding and desolate and empty; shabby wooden watchtowers that looked like remnants of a lost civilisation, presiding like scarecrows over the solemn expanse; outhouses and logpiles; miniature roadside chapels where motorists could chant out their rosaries whilst a plastic Virgin Mary looked on from behind an eternally illuminated cage; and high up on the mountain, standing out amongst the rash of dark trees, one could make out farmhouses and hermit's hovels, completely at the mercy of the boulders and the lightning. All that separated us from these scenes of muted and mutilated misery was the road, which cut through the land like an indifferent imposition from another world.

'It's not right to keep them like this,' I muttered without much conviction. This was met with silence; a silence that persisted for a long time, until it was broken by a low moan that came from the boot – a noise which none of us had ever heard a pig make before, and sounded for all intents and purposes like a death rattle. We were driving through the biggest village in our valley now and Father pulled into the supermarket car park.

Mother got out, opened up the boot and started screaming like she was fresh out of a fairytale: 'The pigs! The pigs! We must water the pigs!'

Then a lot of things happened at the same time and very quickly. Two of the piglets bolted out of the boot, bringing pandemonium to bear on the car park, whilst the remaining piglet languished in the car, apparently incapacitated by dehydration. Father chased after the two fugitives, and Mother ordered me into the shop to fetch water for the straggler. Car horns blared, children bleated and Father filled the air with his curses. I muddled my way through the carnage and into the supermarket and explained what I could to an assistant who ended up being very helpful in the end, even though she looked at me like I was a lunatic (which I suppose was fair enough). She filled up a bucket in the staff toilet sink and gave it to me and I hurried out, sloshing the cool water down the side of my leg more than I might have on a colder day. Mother wrested the bucket from me and doused the suffering piglet with half its contents. Steamy vapours rose up from the piglet, and it whimpered slightly. Its skin looked like it was halfway to becoming bacon. Mother then trickled the rest of the water into the creature's quivering mouth.

'I told him not to take it! That swindler Baumgartner offered him the runt and he couldn't help himself. I knew it would bring nothing but trouble. I told him not to take it!'

Father had succeeded in capturing one of the stray piglets and stood holding it under his left arm, caught in two minds whether to suspend the pursuit and dump this one off now, or keep a hold of it whilst making straight for the other. When he saw that the other piglet was being pursued by some other agricultural-looking men, he sprinted towards us and bestowed the rooting hog into my unwilling arms.

'Take this, will ya.'

It shuffled and rolled and kicked me in my chest but I latched onto it like it was my own flesh and blood, and I knew then that things would start getting better before they got worse again. Its skin was red-hot and gave me a headache. I did not bother to take a look around me because I knew it would make me upset and I was being merciful to myself. Mother continued to nurse the pig, whose whimpering got fainter and fainter. Father at length returned, but he had no pig to hand.

'Those cheeky fuckers, they nicked one of my piglets! I can't believe it!'

Mother waited for him to collect himself.

'*Schatzi*,' she said.

'What?' said he.

She glanced at the car. 'The pig is dead.'

*

It was a sombre car ride home. We were down to our last pig, and it felt wrong to shove it back in the boot with its deceased sibling, but there was no other way. We left the windows open out of hygiene and respect. I had seen enough that day cool off my overactive imagination – real life had been phantasmagorical enough – and I sat silently in the car, letting time age me. And after time had exacted its toll, we pulled up into the driveway of the old farmhouse, and I felt the same commingling of recognition and alienation which is the essence of any homecoming. When the car was parked, Father turned and looked at me, though I did not look back.

'Well, you know how it is: you leave with two and a half pigs and you come back with one.'

Then he started to laugh. To this day I still don't quite know why.

Daniel Souza

"I want some squash." A command rather than a wish from Adela as she heads for the farmhouse. Lucy scrambles up after her, abandoning the scorched grass.

Adela's mother turns from the large wooden kitchen table, her white hands a benevolence in a bowl full of flour and butter. She wets the pastry leaves to decorate the top of a meat pie. Adela and Lucy take the first few gulps of the orange squash. Adela, in a trance, gazes on the items on the kitchen walls. At her age they appear as vast, dusky yellow plaster frames holding sepia photographs of grandparents along with some dead Victorian relations. Once tea is over and the washing up done Adela's mum will recite the litany of names and titles, Uncle William, Great-aunt Mary, and so on. An old-fashioned copper bedpan attached to a long stick is never taken down. A colander like a dead eye, on a hook. A mop tied with a piece of string to another hook, used most days on the floor after the men have dirtied it with their boots. Near to the ceiling a long gun, slung at an angle on two leather holders, for Daddy to shoot the blasted rabbits.

"Come on now you girls, I need some raspberries for tea. Get a bowl 'Dela, and one for Lucy."

Adela pouts, makes slow deliberate steps to the big wall cupboard. Moving close to Lucy and smirking, she hands her a small white bowl, sticks her tongue out at her friend.

Lucy scowls, a trapped mouse. Adela's mum is occupied, her back turned to them as she washes up. Lucy holds out her hand, her elbow glued to her white blouse. Fearing expulsion, she will not expose herself to her friend's mother.

#

They begin by picking out the ripe berries at the nearest edge of the thicket.

"Go in there. I'll pick these." Adela looks away from Lucy.

"I can't." Lucy's cheeks are red with heat; ruby red stains from over ripe berries smudge her hands, her white legs exposed in grey shorts.

"You're smaller."

Lucy inches into the clump a little way, twisting as if she can avoid the prickled stems. She places a few berries into the bowl. In between the stems Lucy's legs are wrapped round each other, spotted with blood, her darting movements grasping a few berries. She returns to the front edge, the path bordered on the other side by runner bean poles. In silence they each fill a bowl.

#

Two girls hardly taller than the dog, all knees and sandals, run here and there in a frenzy, round the grass square, kicking up dust from the dry patches until Adela falls flat. Lucy follows. One eye open, tongue hanging out, in the shadow of a high brick wall that shelters the apple and pear trees on the other side, the dog watches. The girls lie still in the late afternoon heat, arms outstretched, not touching. They shut their eyes against the light.

The passing tractor rumbles, a regular disturbance the girls ignore. Adela's father brings the tractor in and out of the Long End field gathering in the wheat, then down the farm yard emptying the grain into the barn. Back and forth all day into the evening while the light and the weather hold.

Adela jumps up, "The see-saw!" A long builder's plank on a large garden roller. "Push down, Lucy, you're not big enough."

Adela stands to let Lucy down with a thud.

Adela lies back down on her stomach, hands cupping her chin.

"Why can't we stroke Gracie?" Lucy leans on the wall, her fists on either side. She has been storing flaming words, scorching words, since the raspberries, her flat chest harbouring a stone.

Adela sits up. "Ovisly you're stupid."

Lucy doesn't move. Adela stands suddenly, turns her head this way and that, upwards as if to God, to the universe, riled by Lucy's stillness. "Stupid!" She jumps up, curves her hands, a loudhailer to her mouth, repeats and repeats the single word, turning again in every direction,

"… stupid, stupid …"

Adela suddenly stops, stands, a hand placed at her waist, feet apart challenging Lucy across yards of grass. Her back flat against the sun-warmed brick Lucy digs her heels into the ground. One cautious hand goes out towards Gracie.

Gracie is so soft all over, black on her back but patches of white on her chest like an apron. A long jaw so you think she's forever smiling. Silky fur, curly in places. She barks but the farm visitors – feed delivery drivers, the cowman, the insurance collector – know she's harmless. *She's nearly three now,* Daddy says, *not as if she's a pup any more.*

"Lucy." Adela, her big blue eyes and corn-coloured hair belie a voice like the minister in the pulpit. "Gracie is a farm dog. She's not a pet. Anyway, she's mine."

Lucy withdraws her hand. A muffled rumble of the trailer being lowered after tipping the grain into the silo. Beyond the fruit trees the drone of a rare passing car.

Then Lucy launches herself at Gracie to encircle her, stroke her, lay claim to her. The dog's weight on its haunches backs into the wall, barks before its creamy fangs grip Lucy's arm, teeth on soft flesh and crunching bone, the dog shaking Lucy, flesh tearing, cries and screams heard in the kitchen, blood dripping on to the parched grass, shrieking from two mouths, a man scrambling down from a blue tractor, a fierce voice calling "Becca, come quick. Now!" A woman in a floury apron running, shouting. The man dashing indoors.

The screaming silenced by a punishing blast.

A dog, eyes blank, lifeless on the grass. Lucy lies like a discarded rag; deep red blotches saturate blue and grey cloth. Adela stands apart, mouth fraught, both hands clutching her ears. She runs to the dog, falls to her knees. "No, no!"

Moira Garland

too tired to eat or undress. March. Crazy
as a hormone-fuelled hare, I dash
along the M4, the M5, always against gravity,
to minister to the needy. Then dad fell
downstairs onto concrete, and Nadia
fell down a different, unfathomable,
precipice.
I'm hungry. By the toaster, head in hands.
Need to get out of here. The A4
to Avebury? The stones might pull
me back. A4: good for sonnets, but
my unwritten poems are exploding.
They need A3. Even A2. No. Scotland
is too far. Something's burning. My hair
is on fire.

Bel Wallace

BUILDING ME

You could start at the bottom
with my misshaped feet and dodgy ankles,
moulded by treks down the cobbles of Humber Street
and the time I was dared to jump off the side gate.

Then there's my knees and pelvis
both cracking in harmony with every step,
forged by summertime picnics in Pearson Park,
spending hours on end with bare knees against the bandstand.

It might be good to add some liquids too.
A splash of blood from the shores of Withernsea,
Scarborough and Bridlington,
and some tears from the rain that fell
when I first got my heart broken.

Moving up, give me a ribcage
made from the netting of an old fishing trawler,
teeth, tongue, breath and lungs filled with air from Hessle Road
and fingertips callused with pints from the Adelphi.

Then to finish, add some decorations.
A cartilage piercing made from the twisted metal
of Spiders nightclub, still welded together by 1970s punks,
a pair of cold eyes made from the salt in the Humber
and a kidney stone to match the goldfish
swimming in the marketplace public toilets.

And to hold me together,
give me a spine the length of the A63.

Joe Spivey

JACK GREEN

I am Jack Green, shadow and shape-shifter,
swinger on cross-trees; I've been teaser, hob,

sometime town-crier, chapman's clerk, fiddler
at Maying, my bow hand itchy for plackets.

I am a forester in the Law's coppices;
disappearing through a magistrate's yawn.

An uncommon commoner, you'd call me.
I have a leg to sparkle the finest hose,

to hang a subtle blade. I know courtesy
of the Italian, French or Spanish sort.

I've been a hero in the Lowland Wars,
flying the Orange. And been badged with wounds.

Or nosed the stink of a hair's-breadth ditch
with a troop of horse circling in the darkness.

And the next night with a Cardinal's whore,
my knapsack stuffed with gold crucifixes.

London! She's my Mecca of mysteries;
port of the wide world, sty of fattest pigs!

I mess down into her lickerish Liberties.
A quick scull over the racing river

empties you into them, your poor penny
in the pursey palm of the boatman.

Heads or tails and you're across the roads,
out of the water. I can feel my tongue loosen

the moment that mud kisses my foot; a fine speech
fluttering in the dovecote of my throat.

What can I hawk to the festival feathers?
I improvise a mask. A lisping Spaniard,

distant cousin of Bishop Winchester?
A poor man's John Dee? A painter from Venice?

I have a monkey who can whisper
a sovereign remedy for the Plague.

She leapt into my arms at Cadiz
with a hook of dates from a galley.

She's seen more of the world than I have;
Cathay, the Indies, Afric and Arabia...

She's bent her thieving little fingers
into every port with some blind spots.

What can't I caper impromptu
to tease coins from a pair of veiled eyes?

Who doesn't skip into any temple
with a devil on their shoulder?

John Andrew

REVIEWS

Eftwyrd by Bob Beagrie
Smokestack Books
ISBN 978-1-739173-06-7 pp 218 £8.99

The context for Beagrie's 200 page poem is outlined in our discussion, above. It is enthralling reading – a cracking good yarn, as well as a masterpiece of linguistic gymnastics. Beagrie's prologue provides a disingenuous account of how this epic poem, set in seventh century Northumbria, came to light, setting the stage for other occasions where the author plays hide and seek with the reader: in a number of places, the fourth wall is broken, as it were – for example at the start of the second section. Here, in a digression from the established pattern of hybrid text on left had page, modern English translation on right, there is a helpful note (p. 32):

> 'If you've been comparing the Modern English version to Oswin's original account you may have begun to tune into the hybrid language, noting equivalences and similarities, reading the text out loud to find phonetic echoes helps too.'

This was, exactly, what I had found; 'hwær timn hitsylf' is more readily understood as 'where time itself' if vocalised, and lexical offerings less familiar to a modern reader ('bánhús for the evocative 'bone-house'; 'i hlysnod' for 'he listens') also become increasingly comprehensible if muttered half aloud. Beagrie's keen ear for vernacular and older versions of language is a constant delight, and I found myself increasingly choosing to fumble through the hybrid language (with the help of a largely dormant knowledge of Anglo-Saxon from nearly fifty years ago, enriched by the useful glossary) rather than rushing to read the Modern English. However you choose to read the poem, the way in which this very non-traditional text engages your attention makes for a unique experience as a reader, in which your participation is honoured and entertained in a unique manner. Taking it slowly enough to learn to be at ease with the hybrid language is, in itself, a fresh experience of how to encounter poetry; a welcome change from the vapid speed and shallowness of so much of modern life.

The story is a page turner, and contains elements of magic realism (how pleasing we have other mermen/maids in this edition of Dream Catcher), history, romance, morality tale, and other genres. There is also a seamless thread of 'othering', as the ill-fated Brother Oswin falls prey to magic spells, is shunned as a 'Polfrocga' or poolfrog (tadpole), is helped to escape, recaptured, threatened with being sacrificed in propitiation for the plague which is sweeping the country at the time of the Synod of Whitby, and finally afforded sanctuary. He attracts suspicion, fear, loathing, as well as desire, compassion, desire, respect.

As you will realise, if you've read my conversation with Bob above, this poem is deeply rooted in histories – and is no less playful for that. Inter-textual encounters recall Bede's sparrow flying in the mede-hall as a metaphor for the ephemerality of life; there are echoes of fairy stories, fantasy novels (and I suspect games and TV series, though these are largely beyond my ken). Yet somehow Beagrie always make you feel utterly in the *present*, questioning your own prejudices and concerns, so that when you raise your head from the page, you feel both bewildered and enlightened. It is hard to do justice to this in a few hundred words; I urge you to buy a copy, to inhabit this very special world, and to join Oswin in his Everyman journey through the vicissitudes of life.

Hannah Stone

A to Z of Superstitions by **Ian Harker**
Yaffle Press
ISBN 978-1-913122-21-8 £7

On receipt of her first collection of poetry, Seamus Heaney wrote to Iggy McGovern in 2005 that the book, 'renders an account and at the same time has a bit of a romp' which very much can be said of Ian Harker's collection. Moreover, Heaney suggested that the book 'Altogether passes the "good crack" (sic) test, a seal of approval that (Derek) Mahon used to require of all slim volumes'. *A to Z of Superstitions* is, indeed, a slim volume but it is fair to say that it too passes the 'good criac test.'

Like his Auntie Vera in the title poem, Harker doesn't

'see things
the way they really are'

and therein lies the joy and craft of the poems in this collection – his ability to take the squint view and to express what he sees vividly are characteristics of the poems. Vera seems well-versed in protective superstitions referencing at one point the walling up of shoes in a house – traditional protection against witches and spirits and the like. Unlike his Aunt, Harker seems less concerned to avail himself of such superstitions and their protective qualities and seems much more keen on welcoming the spirits, ghosts and descendants that populate many of the poems here.

It was Freud who first identified the concept of 'wishful psychosis' whereby, in grief, people wilfully conjured visions of the departed. If Freud thought this a problem, Harker seems not to as several poems appear to be linked to the death of people close to the poet. There is a sense of personal loss but always the emotional content is cleverly evoked and never sentimental. In 'Aortic stenosis (operated)' a dead granddad won't be missed because his presence is still all around, he is slates on the roof, blackbirds, magpies 'but most of all he will be sparrows'. Again in 'Proceed to survivors' a victim of drowning has never really gone away:

'Whenever my arms feel empty,
I remind myself that the drowned
are everywhere, that I can hold him
any time I like…'

Of course this is bittersweet and again Harker controls perfectly the emotional heft:

'I'm pouring him out of his clothes
I'm falling through him like a diving bell …
Every time I cry
I can taste him on the tip of my tongue.'

Though a shortish collection, there are dead dogs, Egyptian mummies taking a stroll in the park, possible suicides, a Dad who names his pets after Leeds United footballers, a clever description of how the angel's share is actually taken from the whisky barrel, and a marvellous evocation of a house still occupied by all those who ever lived in it – shape-shifting on steroids! Harker has a powerful imagination and observational skills; he seems to occupy

'one of those still points
of the turning world'

('Planet-shine') from which vantage point he acutely observes the everyday world and transforms it into something special.

This is an excellent collection – focused, crafted, surreal and bottomed firmly in the realities and possibilities of living a life in a singular place that is, as my Irish family would put it, a 'thin place'. All you need do is stand still with 'everyone you ever loved falling past the window' (Wortley Heights).

Patrick Lodge

***In Search of a Subject* by John Short**
Cerasus Poetry
ISBN 979-8-868453-25-0 (no price given)

The cover image and the title may put some readers off this collection. Neither does it justice. I enjoyed reading *In Search of a Subject* in one day, following its biographical development and recreation of places and characters. I then reread the poems more carefully. While the poet may have spent his life 'in search of a subject' there is a clear subject in all these poems. Nor is the collection as dark as the cover suggests.

John Short has been writing for a long time, and his list of Acknowledgements is impressive. His poems are well crafted but deceptively so. They seem conversational, but every word is carefully chosen, and imagery, structure and rhythm are fitted to the themes. There is a strong sense of place; the poet making us 'see' scenes through telling phrases rather than descriptions. He catches characters' voices and the sounds of places. The pervading atmosphere is one of poverty: from 1950's austerity and then living rough or working for poor wages. But material wealth is not everything as the cultural richness of the last poems demonstrates.

The first section, 'Late Sun' was the most memorable for me. Here, the poet draws on his memories of youth in a 50's small town, and of student life in Leeds. I recognized areas I knew. The title of the second section, 'Endless Travel' sums up Short's life after graduation. These poems are full of light and foreignness, and the voices of characters met during travels. They tend to be a bit sporadic, like his travels, and some do not have the same intensity as the early ones. In the third section, 'African Rice', he captures the atmosphere and vibrancy of different cultures. These poems are set in hot countries, contrasting with the even greater drabness of modern Britain. They round the collection off neatly.

It is hard to extract individual lines as the poems work as a whole. The first section begins as a sequence. 'Liverpool 1946' is a sensitive recreation of his parents' courtship, while 'The Visitor' captures a character from memory. 'Ursulines' conveys the atmosphere of his convent school but is fair in its assessment of a painful memory.

> 'So, I don't bear them grudges,
> it wasn't their fault, just the times…

'Like Detectives' reminds us of the Saturday cinema shows for children.

> 'On the bus home excited
> upstairs while our mothers talked
> adult through Woodbine clouds …'

The title poem, 'In Search of a Subject', conveys the sense of being different which many poets experience:

> 'Not from here, nor there;
> not middle-class or worker,
> and wrong accent…
>
> Enamoured of the pen
> from an early age…'

The colour and atmosphere of later poems is appealing, as in 'Endless Travel, Seville to Kurdistan':

'At chiaroscuro dawn,
farewell to a narrow street
deep inside the blue mosaic city …'

or 'Night Ritual: Gascony':

'Lamps attract a carnival
of airborne life,
we breathe vegetable dusk
down stag beetle lane.'

France, Spain, Kurdistan, Greece, Africa are all recalled with deft touches. The sudden jolt of being back in the UK is conveyed well in 'Winter Light' and 'Biscuit Factory', the latter using sound to good effect:

'The thunderous megalomania
of machinery means action,
dismissing tinnitus as collateral.'

There are tender poems too, especially in the third section, like 'Love Poem':

'I love the cool simplicity of you
that you're not complicated…'

There is a lot going on in this collection which will merit several readings.

Pauline Kirk

Games of Soldiers by Mary Michaels
Sea Cow
ISBN 978-0-950672-96-0 pp53 (no price given)

Described as 'poetic prose vignettes', these texts intrigue from the get-go. Boundaries wobble, there may be the illusion of a narrative thread but that is just a ploy to hook the reader, and tug them in a different direction. The five uneven length sections of 'Dogs, Cats' starts with a dog on the beach, and then introduces us to 'Callum' (who has both a cat and a wife, at least initially) but what snags your interest are the playful digressions into linguistic texture which nod at the surreal: 'Her action with the fork creates an intolerable confusion of categories – like crayfish or bat – impossible to countenance.' The sections shift between first, second and third person, creating an illusion of looking at life through a kaleidoscope.

Michaels' rapid switch of focus within poems and her dispassionate recording of situations has something filmic about it, or even photographic, as there is a quiet stillness in her observations: from the title poem, we move from disturbing human behaviour to gazing at a ripening berry, and questioning

'… If I twist it gently will it come off the stalk?

Maybe not quite yet. When the ants, alerted by some signal
that I can't detect, turn up and colonise, that will be the time.

The ants say it's ready.'

This has shifted our attention away completely from the masculine micro-aggressions of the opening sections to something more contemplative. She draws on 'Iago' and 'Othello' as implicit metaphors for what is being experienced, but it is the minute observation of the 'Tiny green insect' that flies onto her hand that she wants us to look at (or is it?). The writing is rarely descriptive, as such, but where it is, the imagery has an almost Metaphysical quality: 'Rotunda' has delicious descriptions of how 'rain overnight' brings 'gastropods' inside, one of whole list of events that happen while it is raining:

'On the hall carpet, a glittering trail in the shape that a thin silver
chain might fall into, if the clasp had broken.'

Gender, environment, aggression, loss, and the ridiculous all make an appearance in her book, which repays multiple readings, if only to try to capture the vast diversity of ideas within each poem. For example, 'Seven Modes' considers hirsuteness, epilation, bee illnesses, 'A dragonfly over a London garden,' an anonymous (thespian?) woman who 'might spend a lot of time in the Academy's library … Or in a corner of the cellar which was used at the theatre to store old props'. These vignettes culminate in a portrait of 'a single mother in a tower block on the edge of a city, with one last cigarette and not enough tampons and no curtains on the window.'

By turns disturbing, celebratory, compassionate and visionary, these poems are consistently well crafted and engaging. A witty, teasing skirmish with life and its languages, this book is highly recommended.

Hannah Stone

All the Eyes that I have Opened by **Franca Mancinelli (translated by John Taylor)**
Black Square Editions
ISBN 978-0-9997028-9-5 $25

Joan Didion once wrote that it took her years to discover that she was neither a good writer nor a bad writer but simply 'a person whose most absorbed and passionate hours are spent arranging words on pieces of paper.' Mancinelli, one of Italy's most exciting contemporary poets, would appreciate that, as the first impression of this bi-lingual version of *Tutti gli occhi che ho aperto* (2020) is the care in which words have been organised on the pages. The poems are short – sometimes discursive, sometimes allusive – and appear in several locations on the pages. There is much blank space throughout the collection but as the quality of poetry is not measured by the kilo or the kilometre this does not matter, especially as Mancinelli sees the spaces, the blankness, in the book as highlighting the importance of silence, in which the subject who writes sacrifices her own individuality to make room for the Other from which the poetry flows.

In an interview with Adele Bardazzi and Roberto Binetti, Mancinelli writes of the lines of poetry as the flights of an imprisoned insect – the line on the page is born when the insect sees a way out, 'heading where it sees more light.' This collection becomes a kind of 'hybridization' between poetry and prose, fragmentary notes and remarks placed "in my notebook as if in a sack of seeds" and given sustenance to develop. Some may find the aesthetics laid out here as obscure or obscurantist but no matter as the poetry is very much redeemed by Mancinelli's exquisite use of language and image – she has noted that much of her work has 'reached' her 'while I was swimming or walking' and this collection has an element of meditative flow in which poetic outcome appears more as teasing koan than anything else. The poems are organised into several sequences which cover collaborations with artists, photographers and writers and focus on refugees, relationships gone wrong and saints. In all cases though Mancinelli is remorseless in her pursuit of a redemptive meaning: if life is a series of small deaths – 'Deaths are time's beads, we go through them like a string' – then her poems are codebreakers seeking to decipher the runes and communicate the positives through her poetry.

The poems are replete with references to seeing as if all may be revealed if you look hard enough. The section on Santa Lucia, patron saint of the blind, who is often portrayed with her gouged out eyes before her, suggests not blindness but Santa Lucia's ability to see with her heart, to illuminate the darkest day:

> 'I look at your eyes on the plate
> grains of a vibrating face
> open like the blue
> over a harvested field.'

Mancinelli's clear gaze 'shatters the surface of reality as would a stone, water.' One of the remarkable themes in this collection is Mancinelli's relationship to the natural world – notably trees. Indeed the title itself derives from an incident when she was walking in the Apennines, 'full of inner devastation,' and an old scarred tree 'came to meet me' and declared 'all the eyes that I have opened are the branches I have lost.' This powerful insight brings together the trees and seeing and the belief that something positive can always be drawn out of the negative. It is not as if Mancinelli simply admires the beauty and fortitude of nature, in the poetry she becomes nature – 'affective biology' she terms it – is rooted and alive and productive:

> 'I am potted
> and possessed. I live in the earth's
> safekeeping, with hands sunk
> like roots at work.'

This is a remarkable collection, not least because of John Taylor's sensitive and graceful translation – no easy matter with a poet whose stock in trade is precise, nuanced and subtle language. These poems are 'like sunrays penetrating entwined branches' – bringers of light and warmth.

Patrick Lodge
(Note: given the nature of the text it is very difficult to give a poem title after a quotation.)

Are You Judging Me Yet? Poetry and Everyday Sexism by **Kim Moore Seren**
ISBN 978-1781726877 pp 206 £9.99

I was delighted to review Kim Moore's *All The Men I Never Married* (which won the Forward Prize for Best Collection in 2022) and *What The Trumpet Taught Me* in Dream Catcher 45, and was not going to miss the opportunity to hear Moore read at the excellent Rhubarb Open Mic held monthly in Shipley. It was compelling listening, and the room was thronged. For a writer of such renown, she has an unassuming presence, but there was no doubt that her work resonated with the audience, and for good reason. This latest book was produced 'in conversation with' *All The Men I Never Married*, and develops the theories and concepts about poetry and everyday sexism which were explored and analysed in her PhD thesis undertaken at Manchester Metropolitan University under the supervision of, among others, Michael Symmons Roberts.

Moore describes the book as 'a reader-directed text', and this articulates itself in a unique format: suggestions are made as to the order in which the seventeen sections of prose, five groups of poems from the companion volume, and two individual poems may be read. Whether you opt for this sort of guided indeterminism or adopt a more conventional 'a' to 'z' journey, this is a fascinating, challenging, brilliant book.

Moore's style as a poet is well attested, but meeting these poems again juxtaposed to the analytical chapters brought them into even sharper focus: this companionship of prose and poetry forced me to ask myself the questions implicit in her invitations at the end of sections, such as:

'If you are still unsure whether sexism exists, turn to 'Sexism is a Slippery and Fluid term' on p. 76.'

Or:

'If your body has ever spoken without you knowing what it said, turn to 'The Body is the Blind Spot of Speech' on p. 145.'

Even these invitations have a lyrical tone, and the scholarship embedded in the analytical chapters is convincing, approachable and feels important to facing up to the elephant in the room which is 'everyday' sexism; the so-called 'micro-aggressions' that damage and distort; the ways in which sexism and racism are interconnected. We are also offered pathways for reading through the identity of a woman or a man or non-binary person.

Reading this book gave me an even deeper respect for Moore for the way in which her learning and authentic engagement with literary, gender and political theory is expressed in such a compelling manner. The prose essays are none of them dauntingly long, and references to further reading are given in the conventional academic manner and are not intrusive. But this is SO much more than a scholarly read. The book starts with fifteen 'variations on an introduction' in a section titled 'Desire Lines'. This was the clue for me: I understand desire lines to be the alternative paths to the ones most often trodden, marking the way individuals have chosen to walk, regardless of mandated routes. This is about a freedom to explore, to find alternatives. Here is a map or guidebook for anyone who wants to wander wilfully through the subject, pleasing themselves as to where they halt, turn back, turn off the route. A rigorous, honest and utterly engaging companion for journeys into gender, sexism and survival, this is a book that will accompany me through me reading and writing.

Moore says:

'I wanted to write a playful, angry, sad, thoughtful, transforming, transformative book – and by reading it you are transforming it once again: for that act of faith I give my thanks.'

I hope her generosity will be rewarded with your attention.

Hannah Stone

The Invisible by Alessio Zanelli
Greenwich Exchange
ISBN: 978-1-910996-71-3 pp97 £11.99

The Italian born and raised Zanelli writes in English, and clearly has spent some time in northern England as there are moors and heather,

Millstone grit and dales, a reference to 'an unusually clear Yorkshire day' and even Cannon Hall Farm amongst the 70 poems of this collection.

These poems strive to wrestle with great themes: time, the universe, cosmology; alongside current events/disasters: the deaths of the astronauts on the Challenger, Ukraine, refugees; as well as a final moving section dealing with death and grief, around the loss of his mother.

'I' and 'me/my' appear in this collection more than is to my taste, acknowledging that this is personal preference and not a critique, as such. Nevertheless, it is a risky business placing oneself in the list of butchered at Wounded Knee ('Reviving Wounded Knee'):

'What's become of Rain-in-the-Face,
Kicking Bear, He Dog, Spotted Elk?
…
I can't help feeling I am one of them…
So, my ghost rides about undaunted,
…although I have never been there.'

As is making claim to the thoughts of the doomed Challenger crew, he seems

'…sure they sought
no fame, just heaven…'

not to mention higher powers: in the final line of 'Principia' (12 lines of 'principles' or 'truths'), he asserts that:

'God does make mistakes, on purpose.'

Nevertheless, there is little doubting the depth and sincerity of the grief felt at the losses in his life, gently and reflectively expressed in the final 10-12 poems.

Overall, the shorter poems make more of an impact, whether through more assiduous editing or a conscious reining in. And in this vein, it might well be that *'Stellar Boff'* proves to be the poem that sticks with me longest, containing as it does, the lines:

'finally aware the whole fkn cosmic shebang
hasn't got the slightest purpose whatsoever'

Amen to that.

Nick Allen

INDEX OF AUTHORS

Andria Cooke 102, 103
Andy Fletcher 73
Anne Eyries 27, 92
Anne Ryland............46, 66, 123
Bel Wallace 86, 131
Bob Beagrie...........9, 10, 11, 12
Carmella de Keyser 121
Clifford Liles 70
Colin Pink.................19, 95, 99
Corbett Buchly 83
Daniel Souza........................124
David Sapp 31, 41
David Thompson 28, 29, 30
Debi Knight 101
Estill Pollock 21, 24
George Jowett.................23, 106
Gerald Killingworth...............80
Graham Mort 13
Greg McGee 1
Greg Smith 82, 84
Guy Jones 57
Hannah Stone ..3, 135, 139, 142
Heather Deckner..................104
Heather Hughes 93, 94
Hilaire 33, 63, 116
Ian Chapman..........................64
Ivan McGuinness.............72, 79
Jagoda Olender 117, 118
James B. Nicola 89, 97
Joe Spivey............................132
John Andrew.................77, 133

Katie Campbell........69, 88, 113
Keith Willson..........................16
Kemal Houghton....................20
Ken Gambles 76
Malcolm Carson 111
Margaret Poynor-Clark..........52
Mark Pearce.........................107
Martha Glaser 53
Martin Reed 62, 74
Michael Newman...................48
Moira Garland 34, 128
Niall McGrath..............105, 110
Nick Allen 144
Noel King 96
Owen O'Sullivan 68, 81
Oz Hardwick..............15, 60, 85
Patrick Lodge...............136, 140
Pauline Kirk.........................137
Phil Connolly...................43, 44
Philip Dunn............................59
Ruth Aylett 18, 65, 75
Simon Haines........................50
Simon Tindale 17, 51, 122
Steve Smith............................38
Stuart Pickford.........47, 78, 120
Susan Sciama.........................61
Terry Sherwood 90, 98
Tonnie Richmond 26
Wilf Deckner 100
William Coniston..........49, 119

INDEX OF AUTHORS

Other anthologies and collections available from Stairwell Books

Goldfish	Jonathan Aylett
Strike	Sarah Wimbush
Marginalia	Doreen Hinchliffe
The Estuary and the Sea	Jennifer Keevill
In | Between	Angela Arnold
Quiet Flows the Hull	Clint Wastling
Lunch on a Green Ledge	Stella Davis
there is an england	Harry Gallagher
Iconic Tattoo	Richard Harries
Fatherhood	CS Fuqua
Herdsmenization	Ngozi Olivia Osuoha
On the Other Side of the Beach, Light	Daniel Skyle
Words from a Distance	Ed. Amina Alyal, Judi Sissons
Fractured	Shannon O'Neill
Unknown	Anna Rose James, Elizabeth Chadwick Pywell
When We Wake We Think We're Whalers from Eden	Bob Beagrie
Awakening	Richard Harries
Starspin	Graehame Barrasford Young
A Stray Dog, Following	Greg Quiery
Blue Saxophone	Rosemary Palmeira
Steel Tipped Snowflakes 1	Izzy Rhiannon Jones, Becca Miles, Laura Voivodeship
Where the Hares Are	John Gilham
The Glass King	Gary Allen
A Thing of Beauty Is a Joy Forever	Don Walls
Gooseberries	Val Horner
Poetry for the Newly Single 40 Something	Maria Stephenson
Northern Lights	Harry Gallagher
Nothing Is Meant to be Broken	Mark Connors
Heading for the Hills	Gillian Byrom-Smith
More Exhibitionism	Ed. Glen Taylor
The Beggars of York	Don Walls
Lodestone	Hannah Stone
Unsettled Accounts	Tony Lucas
Learning to Breathe	John Gilham
Throwing Mother in the Skip	William Thirsk-Gaskill
New Crops from Old Fields	Ed. Oz Hardwick
The Ordinariness of Parrots	Amina Alyal
Somewhere Else	Don Walls

For further information please contact rose@stairwellbooks.com

www.stairwellbooks.co.uk
@stairwellbooks